The DREAM Power Goal System: Five Simple Steps to Achieve Any Goal, Guaranteed!

Monica M. Regan

DREAM Power Goal System: Five Simple Steps to Achieve Any Goal, Guaranteed

ISBN 10: 0-9831698-8-8
ISBN 13: 978-0-9831698-8-8

Published by: Expert Author Publishing
http://expertauthorpublishing.com

Canadian Address
1265 Charter Hill Drive
Coquitlam, BC, V3E 1P1
Phone: (604) 941-3041
Fax: (604) 944-7993

US Address
1300 Boblett Street
Unit A-218
Blaine, WA 98230
Phone: (866) 492-6623
Fax: (250) 493-6603

What Others Say About This Book

The DREAM Power Goal System is not just another dry self-help book. It covers every aspect of how to achieve all of your most important life goals while being highly interesting and entertaining. Monica Regan weaves in her own stories and experiences to provide a realistic application of this system that keeps you reading and inspired. As a professional, business and life coach, I have read and researched extensively on goal setting and achievement, and The DREAM Power Goal System is simply a brilliant manual for how to achieve any goal! All the tools are there and they are highly effective. If you want to create results in your life, read this book!

Lisa Princic, Entrepreneur Coach
www.changemakerstoolbox.com

Despite its simplicity and straightforward approach, the DREAM Power Goal System is an effective and indispensable guide for anyone who wants to set and achieve goals. The steps in this book will support you in starting to live the life you always wanted for yourself. Not only does Monica clearly explain each of the steps well, she illuminates them with engaging examples of how they can be applied in everyday life.

Matthew Chan CA, AMP, MBA
www.mortgageplan.ca

Monica Regan has done something very rare. She has written something based in great knowing without sounding like a know it all. Her writing is not arrogant and detached, it is written with warmth and kindness and from the fingertips of somebody who has been there and struggled and come out the other side. It's an effective pragmatic approach with a compassionate touch. This book is not about big picture philosophies, it is a detailed, specific, and step-by-step guide to getting what you want.

Daniel Packard
Social Acupuncturist
Dating and Relationship Expert and Coach

There isn't a person I know who wouldn't benefit in some way from reading this book. It takes concepts many readers on a spiritual path or journey of personal growth are already familiar with, and neatly ties them together with a bow. Never underestimate simplicity, it is often the simplest concepts that are the most profound and most effective. If you use just one of the concepts in this book, you will change your life for the better.

J Isaac
Co-Founder, Ecotize It!

Ever wondered why you aren't creating the results you want, even when you've tried setting goals in the past? Author Monica Regan has brought the methodology of achieving dreams down to a few simple, powerful steps that anyone can understand and follow.

Nora Weber
President TerraCom Communications Group

Monica Regan humanizes the goal achieving journey by using examples of her own struggles, resistance, breakthrough moments and successes. The DREAM technique is a step-by-step process that any person at any stage in their life could benefit from. Monica Regan has written this book as if she is sitting next to you speaking to you as a coach, guide, confidante and cheerleader. I know that each time I read this book, whether it be the fifth time or the tenth time, I will learn something new and continue growing and challenging myself.

Erin Davis
Social Service Worker

I have had the pleasure of working with Monica to set and achieve, several goals. This book is an excellent guideline to achieving all of your DREAMS, all you have to do is read it and take action. I use the principles outlined in this book everyday to achieve my goals, whether they are spending more time at my summer estate, traveling to new exotic locations, supporting my family, growing my businesses or supporting people in achieving what they say they want in life. When you are ready to get what you say you want, read this book and get it done. It does not have to be hard, you deserve everything you want in life.

Derrick Smith, CEO and Founder
Deadfrog Brewery
www.Deadfrog.ca

For Vancouver PLD Team 15

Acknowledgments

To my father, who taught me that the universe is never-ending. You sparked off, in an eight-year-old's mind, a sense of curiosity that has sent me on a thirty (plus!)-year journey of both the inner and outer universe.

To my mother, who constantly modeled ceaseless commitment, integrity and hard work, to you I owe the value I hold in these qualities, without which I would have never found the discipline and dedication required to create DREAM Power.

To my brother, whose single-minded focus and determination could not have been more of a yin to my yang of a meandering and scattered existence, from you I learned the definition of success.

To Lisa, with whom I first began to analyse the world in the Westview parking lot, your profound influence on me can never be overstated. Thank you for your courage and for pushing harder than anyone I know.

To Laura, my LS Sister, you have taught me that a little pain now can mean a lot of pleasure later. I have learned that this causes a lot less suffering than my long-standing history with play-now-pay-later thinking and, again, it is one of the reasons this book came to be.

To LB Seminars, thank you for providing me with the opportunity to know that I am a deserving, dynamic, beautiful woman committed to creating loving relationships in my life, now! Ana, Paul and Littley, there is no question that you know exactly how much of your influence is in these pages.

To Xipi, who, in eight days, shared with me the meaning of fidelity, truly unconditional love and how to laugh so hard that my legs stopped working. You changed how I see the world and I am still grateful to you all these years later.

To Huub, who taught me that nothing lasts, nothing is lost, everything only changes. You will never know how deeply those words affected me.

To Tim, who has always had never-ending, categorical support and belief in me, you live the life of your dreams and for that you inspire me.

To Bob Burnham, who was the absolutely perfect person to attract into my life, and who came at the absolutely perfect moment. Your wisdom and encouragement brought out the best in me and, in turn, in this book.

And finally to that other Bob, the creative mind that inspired the cover design. Your technical knowledge, cheeky humour, crooked smile and opening heart have brought tremendous lightness and light to my life. Thank you for your unquestioning support, for the "skinniness" and for the delight of laughter to bring down my "eye walls" and take it all a little less seriously.

To all of you, my heart is overflowing with gratitude. Thank you, thank you, thank you.

Contents

Introduction

You have picked up this book because you are someone who wants success. You want to be, do or have something greater in your life than what you are, do or have right now. Whether it is financial, creative, health, relationship or community related, there is something you dream of and you have not been able to, or do not know how to, create it. You want to achieve your dreams and have given up, or you do not know where to start. Maybe you don't even know exactly what it is that you want, and you just know that you want more.

What is the secret to being, doing or having anything that you choose? How can you create the life of your dreams? You will learn the secret in this book. By using the DREAM Power Goal System you will learn how to achieve any goal you have. And it starts with only one thing. What is the single best predictor of someone's success? The answer may surprise you. It is simply: goals. Napolean Hill, who interviewed over five hundred successful men and women in the early part of the twentieth century, found that one of the most significant threads that linked all of these highly successful people was whether or not they set goals. Goal-setting books have been published by famous authors such as Brian Tracy, Tony Robbins and Zig Ziglar. The Harvard Business School publishes books on goals. Goal books are written for relationships, finances, business, weight loss and athletic peak performance, and the list goes on. There is little doubt of the effectiveness of goal setting. Though goal setting alone does not create results, goal setting is a very, very powerful and effective step, and goal setting is the first step in getting exactly what you want.

And yet the vast majority of the population does not set goals. Keith Ellis, author of The Magic Lamp: Goal Setting for People Who Hate Setting Goals, admits that for years, he read everything he could get his hands on about setting goals — and then he simply never set one. Many of us understand that setting goals is very effective but we resist doing it.

Or, perhaps, you are how I used to be and set goals but don't seem to ever actually achieve them. You got excited, figured out what you wanted and within a few weeks the goal faded into frustration. Maybe you pretended that you never even set it so that you would not have to deal with the fear that you did not have what it takes to achieve it. Maybe you have gone through this experience more than once, and now and you are at the point of not even setting goals at all anymore. The disappointment and frustration of failed goals may have turned to apathy or even self-loathing.

I have been there. By thirty-four years old, I was a qualified teacher; had a degree in psychology; obtained a diploma in fine arts; had lived in London, Mexico and Quebec and had backpacked through many more exotic locations. And I was at the lowest point of my life. Despite what appeared to be a rather glamorous existence of travel and living abroad, I was single, unhealthy, unemployed and in significant debt.

Essentially, I had lived a life of spontaneity, following whatever whim took my momentary fancy and paying for most of those whims with a credit card. I avoided looking at the credit card bills for months at a time and just paid minimums each month. When the next bright, shiny object or opportunity came along (read: clothes, cocktail nights out, more clothes, multiple month-long trips to multiple destinations in Central America, Europe, Asia …), I either convinced myself that I didn't owe as much as I thought I did or that I would find some sort of money guru to sort out my finances with his miracle repayment plans. I may have even let a few marry-a-rich-man fantasies slip in there. Ten years of this, and you can imagine the hole I had dug myself.

My latest escapade had included relocating myself to the other side of Canada for a relationship with a man I had been involved with for little more than a month. It was a relationship that I desperately wanted to work but that was destined to end in a spectacular explosion of pain and anger. Licking my wounds, I had retreated home to Vancouver, jobless, broke and lonely.

And there I was, living in a dark, chilly, 400-square foot basement suite where I was occasionally visited by a rat. As I child, I had dreamt that, by the time I was thirty-four, I would be a married career woman, living with a white picket-fenced-in house with two kids, a dog and my smart and sexy husband. Nope. I was living alone, without a job, and was finding rat turds in my cereal boxes.

This was not supposed to be how educated, modern women lived! I comforted myself with the fact that the job market was tough and that I had had a lot of fun travelling and living a very free life in my twenties. I also comforted myself with lots of nachos and ice cream because no matter what story I told myself about why my choices were justifiable, I was full of shame and felt completely out of control.

I was longing for the life I had always wanted. I was constantly confronted with friends who had it together with their husbands, careers, babies and bodies. I was too embarrassed to tell them about my dire financial situation. I was jealous that they were not alone and I was. I didn't want to be around them but I didn't want to be on my own either.

After numbing out the tightness and the burning anxiety in my chest each night with food and TV, I woke up with a feeling of dread in my stomach. Add to that the disgust I felt at my caloric stuffing down of emotions and numbing of my thoughts with mindless sitcom drivel, and I could hardly bear to be in my own company. I escaped to a local coffee shop every morning to read as an excuse to get out of my little apartment and forget about how terrible I felt. After I was well hopped up on caffeine and felt I had more than out-welcomed my stay, I would walk home with the slowly building angst in my stomach about looking online for seemingly non-existent jobs. During those months I filled out dozens of job application packages and never heard back from a single one.

And then, finally, there was a little light at the end of the tunnel. A woman who ran a company that went into schools to teach a gymnastics program hired me on a trial basis, as I was a qualified teacher. What I conveniently failed to mention to her was that physical education was my absolute least favourite subject to teach and that I myself had failed P.E. when I was in school. Kids in seats? No problem, I could manage that. Kids running in open spaces, in all different directions, with the objective of flinging their bodies onto apparatus that vaguely resembled torture devices? Big problem. I could not manage that. I got fired.

I thought I was down before getting fired from a low-paying job that I took out of sheer desperation, but I had no idea how much further down I could go. Nachos and ice cream did not even make me feel better anymore.

In the depths of my self-pity, sobbing on my landlord's shoulder, I blubbered,

"I just want to hear someone say, 'Congratulations, Monica! You got your dream job! It is everything you wanted and more!'" And that was when I decided I would hear that. I would hear someone say it to me every day.

I woke up in the morning, and I sat up and mentally pictured a family member or friend patting me on the back, shaking my hand or hugging me and saying that exact phrase: Congratulations, Monica! You got your dream job! It is everything you wanted and more!

After a few days of this, it dawned on me that I did not exactly know what my dream job was. I had been so busy looking for anything and thinking in terms of desperation that I simply thought it would be crazy to focus on my dream job because it probably didn't even exist!

It became clear that I felt that if I said what my dream job was, I would limit myself to only that job and then would miss another good job. That was when it occurred to me that if I started with the assumption that my dream job didn't exist, it was pretty unlikely I would ever find it. That is when I decided to set a goal of getting my dream job. What was the worst that could happen? I was already unemployed and about as far away as I could get from a dream job! I had nothing to lose.

I started to get really specific. I wrote down everything I wanted — the grade level, location, salary, benefits, type of contract, type of staff to work with, most suitable school philosophy and the ideal boss. I began to think about that job each morning after I heard myself being congratulated for getting it. And I kept searching and applying.

Eventually, I came across an ad for a job that was a temporary contract. It did not fully hit the mark but it was pretty close to most of what I had written down. The application closing date was the next day, so I put together the application package (which required several hours' work) and dropped it off about ten minutes before the closing time!

I heard nothing for a month and figured that, like the dozens of other packages I had dropped off, it was on the bottom of some pile and another grinning teacher was shaking hands and being congratulated. However, I kept my chin up and continued hearing my own congratulatory phrase in my mind, determined to make it a reality.

About six weeks after I dropped off the application, my phone rang. It was that school calling me in for an interview. I prepared like a mad woman, calling teacher friends to do mock interviews with me, adding to my portfolio and pulling out my crispest suit to wear.

As I was led into the office where the interview was to take place, I was told that I was not being interviewed for the position that I had applied for and that they had already filled that position. The interviewers went on to describe the position I was being interviewed for. It was exactly what I had written down with even better benefits.

I was dumbfounded.

But not so dumbfounded that I was unable to pull off a great interview. I was offered the job almost immediately. As soon as the Assistant Head teacher called to invite me to work for them, I called my dad to tell him the news and the details of the position. Can you guess what he said to me?

"Congratulations, Monica! You got your dream job! It is everything you wanted and more!"

That experience was so uncanny and so incredibly powerful that I began to analyse it and think about what it was that worked so beautifully. Then I began to read and take courses about goal setting and achievement, and also about concepts like visualization, the Law of Attraction and metaphysics. I started setting and achieving dream goals for myself, like purchasing my first home. I used it for leadership goals, such as being selected to go to Africa to work in partnership with the Ugandan Ministry of Education and the Jane Goodall Institute to implement environmental education into the curriculum. I continued to gather evidence and anecdotes and to practice and apply everything I was learning about achieving goals and visions for my life, until I came up with a system that I could apply to anything I wanted.

I share that system with you here in this book. The DREAM Power Goal System for achieving what you want from life is the culmination of everything that I have learned and used to achieve my dream goals. This system works. Whether it is relationship, financial, health, wealth or community related, you will achieve whatever dreams you have if you put this system into place. It works. Every time. Guaranteed. You, simply, must do the work.

DREAM Power

Decide.

Realize.

Energize.

Action.

Maintain Momentum.

DREAM
Decide!

The most important thing about goals is having one.
-Geoffry F. Abert

What Do You Want?

What *do* you want? This is a crucial question. It is the most important question we can ask ourselves. Most people have some vague sense of what they want, and it usually starts with more money, less stress and increased happiness. But a surprising number of people cannot get any more specific than that when first asked. Most of us have never sat down and actually asked ourselves specifically what we want. This is, in fact, really surprising once we think about it.

Most of us have dreams, but we keep them somewhere in the backs of our minds. Often we frame them as fantasies. We wrap all kinds of limiting thoughts around them like: *that would be a dream of mine, one day* and *it would be nice if I could* . . . But we often never actually take any steps toward turning these dreams into a reality. We are content to live our lives on autopilot, reacting to the circumstances that come to us instead of being the designers of our lives.

We have tremendous power to turn our dreams into reality. But we don't. We don't realize how powerful we really are. We may not even dare to imagine that we could truly have the life of our dreams. But what if you did imagine the life of your dreams? Is this life possible for you?

Imagine what your life would be like if you knew exactly what you wanted and you had the tools to make it happen. How exciting would your life be if you had a clear view of what you wanted and how you were going to get there, as well as the knowledge that you had everything you needed available to you to create this life? This is absolutely possible.

It is ok if you don't have a clear view of what you want. If you already know exactly what you want, you are in the minority of people and you are in a very good position to start achieving your goals and dreams with the tools in this book. But, again, it is ok if you don't. The **D** in **DREAM** is to support you in **D**eciding what you want.

So how do you figure out what you want? How do you **D**ecide? Are you ready for the answer? This is a big one! Here it is: You ask yourself. That is it.

Take five minutes now, in an environment where you will not be interrupted, and write down a list of everything you would like to have, do or be in your life. Even if you have some clear ideas about what you want in your life, still do this activity. This is important. You may be tempted to think that you will read the whole chapter (or even the whole book) and then come back and do this activity. Do not fall into this trap. If you want something different in your life, then you have to *do something differently.* Do it now.

As you begin to write, do not edit yourself. Do not allow yourself to refrain from writing something down because it seems unachievable or vague or completely out of your comfort zone. Do not tell yourself you will never have the time or you will never have the money. Just write down whatever you want. Notice if you feel anxious as you write down some of the bigger things that you want and write them down anyway. It is just a list.

Once you have a list in place, read it over and notice how you feel as you look at each item on the list. Do you feel excited? Nervous? Energized? Fearful? Giddy? You may find you feel all of these things at different items. You may also feel nothing. These are all perfectly normal reactions. Some items on the list may be terrifying because your mind immediately begins to imagine the risk involved in creating these things. Some may get your engines roaring, making you feel ready to go right now! Notice how they make you feel and allow yourself to just feel that passion, nervousness, anxiety or butterflies in your stomach.

Once you have your list, separate the things you came up with into three categories. The first category is non-tangibles. Non-tangibles are things that we know we have achieved because we will *feel* them. These would include things like:

* *To be happier*
* *To feel more loved and appreciated*
* *To have more passion in my life*

* *To make a difference in the world*
* *To improve my self-confidence*

The second category consists of your dreams. These are the things that we fantasize about the most with the phrase, "One day I would love to …" They include things like:

* *Sail around the world*
* *Buy my dream house*
* *Travel to Paris*
* *Work at the UN*
* *Open my own specialty wine store*
* *Publish a novel*
* *Become a doctor*

Finally, you can put the remaining items in the third category as goals. Goals are generally the stepping-stones to achieving either your non-tangibles or your dreams. Your list of goals may include things like:

* *Quit smoking*
* *Lose 15 pounds*
* *Improve my relationship with my son*
* *Pay off my debt*
* *Find a partner*
* *Learn to belly dance*
* *Volunteer with Amnesty International*

Now you have a list of what you want. This is your starting place. It may change, grow or shrink as time goes on, but having an actual written list of things that you want is the first step. Notice that your goal category is generally steps to creating your non-tangibles or to creating your dreams. You may wish to become a volunteer with Amnesty International because it serves as a stepping-stone toward your dream of working at the UN, which in turn supports that non-tangible of making a difference in the world.

Not all your lists will line up as neatly with each other as *volunteer with Amnesty International* linking with *work at the UN* linking with *make a difference in the world*, but what you will notice is that there is usually some kind of link. Pay attention to those links. Do you notice any patterns between the three categories? They can help you zero in more closely on what you really want out of life. When you find these links, notice how you feel as you think about the goal, the dream and the non-tangible desire. If you feel excited, energized, empowered or passionate, you have stumbled onto something big. Your feelings are always a clue to figuring out what you really want.

Get In Balance

When I first began to work on achieving my goals, I too struggled with figuring out what I wanted. I just followed my nose, falling into this or that, because it happened to be in my path. The first time I went to write down my goals, I ended up with a very long list of scattered ideas and momentary inspirations, without any real focus, about what I would like to have, do or be. Then I felt overwhelmed at the idea of having to figure out how I was going to do all of these things, and my nice, long list ended up as a page in a journal on a bookshelf in my closet. You are already one step ahead of this. Your aspirations are organized into categories that we can begin to work with. Our next step is to figure out which ones make the most sense for you to work with now.

One way to help you decide which goals you want to work on first is to look at the balance in your life. Often we are very highly achieving in some areas, while others are left to the wayside. A commonly used tool for understanding where we may be out of balance is called the Wheel of Life. Each section in the wheel represents one of the main areas that we spend our energy on.

Often, we put a lot of energy into some areas, and work hard to create success in those, while neglecting others. When we put equal energy into each area, we are far more likely to feel at peace. Using this Wheel of Life to see where you may be neglecting your attention can help you **Decide** on where to set your goals.

Most of these are pretty self-explanatory, but the Spiritual Connection category may need a little further explanation. This is where, in your life, you give to others and/or connect with your own inner power, whether that is religious, new age, metaphysical or simply trusting your intuition or gut. The Sense of Community and Leadership section can translate to volunteerism, becoming a vegetarian, becoming more committed to a church, taking on leadership roles in a career, learning to meditate, sitting on a board in the community and so on. It is an area that is often neglected in our society but increases people's levels of life satisfaction and balance when attended to.

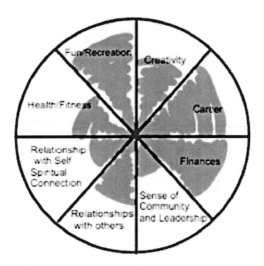

Here is an example of a completed wheel. The area where the circle is filled in the least represents the lowest level of satisfaction in that area. The area where the circle is filled in the most represents the highest level of life satisfaction in that area. Once you have filled in your own wheel, it may become apparent where you want to focus on starting with your goals.

I recommend you work on no more than three goals at a time, but you may feel one is enough to get started. If you have an area that you notice is out of balance, that is a great area to set your goal from. Look over your goals and begin thinking about which ones will serve you best right now.

Dare to Decide on Big Goals

The dreams we have often remain just that: dreams and not reality. You were asked to write your dreams and desires down, regardless of the reasons why you thought that you might not be able to achieve them. You may well have been quietly thinking in the back of your mind, "Ok, I will be a good student and write it down but I *know* this is a pipe dream. There is no way it could ever *really* happen."

Or, you may have found yourself very anxious when you wrote down your dreams. You may also have noticed as you wrote down those dreams that, despite my encouragement for you *not* to do so, you edited yourself. Again, this is a very normal reaction to stating your dreams.

Dreaming big takes courage because we have become very comfortable with what we believe about ourselves. People generally have beliefs about themselves (though usually not in their conscious awareness) that include what they are capable of and what they deserve in life. These beliefs are very strong and, because they are mostly subconscious, we do not realize that we hold them. Our patterns of behaviour will align themselves with these beliefs consistently, unless we spend a little time challenging them. Challenging your unconscious beliefs about yourself can feel rather uncomfortable, which is why we can feel anxious when we set out big goals.

As you noticed your emotional reactions to the goals and dreams and desires you wrote down, you were being given a key to unlock some of your self-beliefs. The more anxious, nervous, fearful or disregarding you felt of the potential for these dreams to become reality, the stronger the hidden belief you have that you do not deserve what you want, that you are not capable enough to create it or to be responsible for it.

These negative reactions are a gift! Most people never take the opportunity to explore these negative self-beliefs and so they set goals and have dreams, but do not get them because their limiting beliefs take over without their ever realizing it.

Overcoming these beliefs does require the willingness to get uncomfortable because our minds will fight to maintain these beliefs. They have been with you a long time and are very comfortable in your neural pathways. The good news is that it is absolutely possible to overcome them. I know because I have done it myself.

I spent most of my twenties without much direction or idea of what I wanted to do with my life. I was working at a local grocery store where I made union wages that were pretty good. I was able to save up enough to do a fair amount of travelling, which had been my way to escape figuring out a path in life. Once on the road, I had so much fun exploring new cultures, wandering without an agenda and meeting other travellers and partying, that I always wanted to stay away longer than I originally planned. I had no real money sense, so I borrowed on credit cards and from other willing lenders. I amassed a rather large debt between those trips and constantly redirecting my educational focus (undergrad in psychology, a few years of art school, acting and writing courses, and on it went—also paid for through loans).

Eventually, I found a path I wanted to follow: I became an elementary school teacher. I also did a lot of self-exploration and taught myself a lot of the principles that are now in this book, which I began to apply to achieve my dreams.

My biggest dream at that time was to own my own home. As I was deeply in debt, this was challenging. I stated the dream because I believed it was important to say I wanted it, but I really did not believe then that it was possible. I did not have any savings and, between paying out on what I owed and knowing that I needed a hefty sum for a down payment, I felt tremendous anxiety about how to move forward.

Though on one had I was committed to the goal, I did everything in my power to avoid working toward it. I began to explore what was behind this resistance and I found that my entire history of getting into debt was linked to the idea that I did not believe I was capable of managing money; it was a belief imprinted in me at a young age.

Once I got clear on this belief that was limiting me, I began to take action and challenge the belief that I was incapable. I was finally able to create the money I needed, find a place I loved and have a signed agreement on the purchase in six weeks! In six weeks I achieved a dream I had not believed was possible for myself.

You are here to live your life. You can live big or small: that is your choice. Have the courage to dream big. Decide on your goals and accept the fears and challenges to get those goals. Overcoming the beliefs that limit those dreams makes us feel empowered, alive and excited about life.

Go back now and look at the goals you have decided to work on. Did you hold back? Did you edit yourself? Did you deny what you really, really want? If you did, change them now. If you do not allow yourself to conceive of it and believe it is possible, you will never achieve it.

Take Leadership of Your Own Life

Remember that the purpose of life is to re-create yourself anew in the next grandest version of the greatest vision ever you held about
Who You Really Are.
-Neil Donald Walsch

When you create goals for yourself, you are taking the first step to leading the direction of your own life. You can now count yourself among the shockingly small 10 percent of people who actually clearly define what they want out of life . Isn't it amazing that the majority of people live their lives and never take any control of the direction that they wish their own lives to go? When you get clear and Decide what you really want in your life, you are taking leadership of yourself.

Life has amazing things to offer us and most of us let it slip by without directing it. We also have amazing things to offer life and many of us are too scared to realize the gifts that we have to offer the world. These are choices! The fear that holds us back from making bold statements about what we want to be, do and have will never serve us. Your goals may seem far away and difficult to achieve, but as you begin to take steps toward them, you will find that what once seemed an insurmountable hurdle is suddenly behind you. You many even find that what you made up about how hard it was going to be in your mind simply never came to pass!

Every step in this process is a choice. Choosing not to lead the direction of your own life is, in many ways, safe and easy. It allows us to not to have to take responsibility for what happens to us; it means that we can blame something outside of ourselves for our circumstances and stay comfortable in our lamenting the lack of money, love, adventure or purpose in our lives.

Taking control of your own life and choosing to lead it in the direction that you want is a powerful process. When you **Decide** what you want, your confidence improves and you feel invigorated, alive and excited. Taking leadership of your life connects you with your values and brings optimism, increased levels of happiness and satisfaction and it models for others someone who is empowered and responsible. Every step that you take in the directions of your dreams will empower you to take the next. Imagine living your life on purpose, creating what you want and being the best that you have to offer the world. That is the journey you are now on. You have decided on your goals. You have decided to take leadership of your life.

Be SMART

Being SMART has nothing to do with intelligence. It is simply an effective goal-framing tool. SMART is a commonly used acronym for framing goals that allows much greater success in your outcomes.

S – Specific

Be specific in how you frame your goal. We often state our goals in non-specific terms such as, "I want to lose weight."

Losing weight is a great goal. It will support your health, enhance longevity and allow you to look the way you wish to. Stating that you want to lose weight is vague and does not give you a clear outcome. A specific weight goal could be, "To be a maximum of 135 pounds".

What is your intended outcome? What exactly would you look like, be like, act like, have or be doing when you achieve your goal? Take each of your current goals and spend a few minutes thinking about exactly what the outcome you want is. Then reword your goals to reflect your desired outcome. This gives you something to hold on to when you are working toward your goal.

M – Measurable

Can you measure your goals? Most goals can be reframed so that you can see exactly what the change will be when you have achieved them. Some goals are easy to measure, such as the goal of reaching your desired weight. Your measure is simply that you have arrived at your desired weight! But others are less simply measured. This is where you must become creative. Let's take the example of having a goal to have a better relationship with your partner. How will you know you have achieved this? What can you use as your benchmark? This is not something that we generally consider measurable, but there are ways to frame even this type of goal as measurable. Here are some ways to reframe this goal into something measurable:

* *I will spend a minimum of two evenings a week with my partner engaged in quality time together.*
* *My partner and I will have signed up for and be attending a cooking (dance, relationship development, etc.) class together.*
* *I will express a kind and loving thought to my partner once a day to show my appreciation of him/her.*
* *I will treat my partner to an extravagance once a week that I would not normally do, each week for 90 days.*

Of course, you can become creative in whatever way you want to create a measurable method for stating your goal. The point is that at the time when you feel you have achieved your goal, you can look back and check to see if you actually did what you wrote down as your measure.

A – Attainable, Achievable

When framing your goals, you may become so excited that you choose a goal that may be ultimately attainable but not in a single step. Remember, your goals are your stepping-stones to your ultimate dreams. It is important to be honest with yourself about what is achievable in each of the smaller steps toward that dream.

Your dream may be to do what you always wanted to do, such as own your own business as a successful clothing designer. All your dreams are achievable. There is simply no question that if you have the belief, desire and intention, you can create it for yourself. Be clear that if you are currently working in a completely unrelated field and have no background in your desired field, stating you will become a successful clothing designer may simply not be attainable in one step. What is achievable for you right now? Perhaps it is taking a design course. Perhaps it is setting up informational interviews with designers to learn some of the things you will need to do to get on your way. Perhaps it is simply to design your first item. Once you have made a currently attainable goal toward your dream and actually achieved it, you simply put the next one in place.

The other side of the attainable coin is to be sure that you are not selling yourself short. Are you setting goals that are worthy of you? Know that as you take steps in the direction of your desires, your confidence grows. Setting a goal that feels pretty big at the outset and requires just a little bit of a stretch to reach means that you will find resources within yourself you may not have previously thought possible. In this way, you will grow, as opposed to choosing something that you know is pretty easily attainable and you just have not gotten around to doing it yet.

R – Risky and Rewarding

First of all, congratulate yourself on already choosing a goal that makes your heart pound. You are on your way to living a bigger life for yourself by just taking the risk of choosing a challenging goal. Your goal must also be rewarding to be motivating. Is your goal something that you dread, not out of that exciting fear of getting out of your comfort zone, but out of its truly being something that you feel you "should" do? Is your goal something that someone else has decided "should" be your goal? If so, trust what is right for you. The truth of whether this is a rewarding goal for you is in your own intuitive sense. You know the answer to this question. If this goal is not rewarding for you, but rather for your father who always wanted you to _____ (fill in the blank), change it.

One hour of life, crowded to the full with glorious action, and filled with noble risk, is worth whole years of those mean observances of paltry decorum.
-Sir Walter Scott

Risk is a word that often has negative connotations. We are taught to avoid it. It implies a possible outcome that is dangerous, painful or potentially causing loss. Risk is the antithesis to comfort. However, we know that when we take risks, we often get greater rewards. In finances, high-risk investments can reap much higher returns. In love, we know that unless we are willing to risk getting our hearts broken, we will never know a true love. Do you remember the first time you approached someone you had a crush on and worked up the courage to speak to them? Your heart was racing, your stomach might have done flips and you may have even fumbled your words and uttered nonsense. But you felt very much alive. You took the chance to put yourself out there in hopes of seeking the attention of that person who made your heart thump and, whether it went in your favour or not, you would have never known had you not done it.

It is so very easy to stay in a place of comfort and safety. Initially, comfort is like being curled up on your favourite chair with a warm blanket. But after a time, comfort and safety breed a numbness that can deaden your soul. Risk is empowering, energizing and exciting. Taking risks builds your confidence and trust in yourself. But risk, for many of us, is understandably terrifying, so we allow complacency or numbness instead.

Of course, at times in our lives, we have all taken risks. Some have led us to great successes and some have caused us great pain. It is those painful experiences, like touching a hot stove, that make us cringe at the thought of doing them again. Take a few minutes to write down the answers to the following questions:

* What are the times in your life when you have taken the greatest risks?

* What successes have you created?

* Where do you know you hold yourself back now from taking risks? Love? Career? Finances? Family relationships?

* What is the price you are paying for holding back?

Review those prices. Who does not get to see the you that is available under the fear that holds you back? Your boss? Your partner? Your children? The people you could be affecting with your new career? You have amazing things to offer this world. Everyone does. We all arrived here with gifts and blessings and many of us keep them inside to the detriment of others. We do this because we are too afraid of the risks that we would have to take to bring that piece of us forward.

Here is my challenge to you: Look one more time at the goals you have chosen to work with. Did you pick safe goals? Did you pick goals that you are telling yourself you want when what you *really* want is the one on your list that terrifies you because of what it means you would have to do to achieve it? Don't sell the world short by staying safe and comfy on your couch. Step up to your life and take on the risky goals. Then notice your heart pounding and your anxiety level rising and be ok with it. You have tremendous power in you to bring the best you forward into this world. Make goals that are a reasonable risk to you.

T- Timely

Putting a timeline on your goal is a very important key to your success. Without a timeline, it is simply too easy to continually say that you get to it later, which is likely why you don't have it already in your life! People who put timelines on their goals have a significantly higher rate of success than those who do not. Your timeline may depend on what your goal is and whether it is a step toward a bigger dream that you have.

A suggestion here would be to set goals that can be created within a maximum of ninety days. Anything longer and the reward becomes too far away to maintain your motivation to move toward it. If you think your goal will take more than ninety days to achieve, ask yourself why. Is it because you will have to get a little uncomfortable to make it happen in that time period? Can you realistically do this in ninety days? What is *really* possible for you? Are you staying safe? I know people who have set goals to make $5,000 in a month. For those people, it was a genuinely risky goal due to the circumstances of their work at the time that they set the goal. I also know people who have set goals to make $30,000 in a month. Those specific people were cheating themselves because that was simply not much of risk for them to state they were going to achieve $30,000 in extra income.

Don't sell yourself short. If the goal is truly unrealistic in a ninety-day timeline, then break it into smaller chunks. What is reasonable and risky in ninety days for you?

Summary

The DREAM Power Goal System starts with Decide

What Do You Really Want?

Make a list and write everything that you can think of. Separate each item into non-tangible desires, dreams and simpler goals. Pay close attention to your positive and energizing feelings as these are clues to what you *really* want. Pay close attention to your negative responses as these are indicators of negative self-beliefs that may hold you back from believing you can achieve a goal.

Get In Balance

Use the Wheel of Life as a tool to help you see where you are out of balance in your life. Consider deciding on goals that help you create more balance. When you are putting your attention equally into different aspects of your life, your sense of peace is increased.

Dare to Decide on Big Goals

It is easy to write out goals that you know you have just been too lazy to get to but that are really not all that big or exciting. Daring to **D**ecide on big goals is exciting, empowering and energizing. Big goals that require you to stretch to achieve them will cause you to butt up against some negative self-beliefs. Overcoming these will create big growth and, in turn, new belief in yourself!

Take Leadership of Your Life

Be among the 10 percent of the population that actually **D**ecide to be in control of their lives by choosing what they want their lives to look like. **D**ecide on your goals for your life. Take ownership and lead your life.

Be SMART

Now that you have a pretty good idea of your goals, begin to ensure that you have SMART goals. **S**pecific, **M**easurable, **A**ttainable/**A**chievable, **R**ewarding/**R**isky and **T**imely.

Now that you have decided on what you want, learn to **R**ealize It!

DREAM
Realize It (In Your Mind First)!

You may think that now that you have finished the first step in the DREAM Power Goal System, **D**ecide, you should begin to take action in the world. But before you take action out there, you must take action inside your own head. You must **R**ealize your goal in your own mind first.

You have decided on your goals. You have put them through the SMART test and tweaked and reworded them accordingly. They are written in stone now, right? Maybe. The very next step to take with your goals is to understand how they affect your mind, because your mind is the single most important secret behind achieving your goals.

You will create the results of your intended goals in your mind long before you create them in the world. It can be no other way. You simply will not create anything that you do not first conceive of in your mind. Nothing you have ever created has not been created first in your mind's eye. To think is to create. This notion has been expressed, in a multitude of ways, by numerous philosophers, metaphysicians, inventors, scientists and teachers, to name a few:

Whether you think you can or that you can't, you are usually right.
-Henry Ford

Imagination is everything. It is the preview of life's coming attractions.
-Albert Einstein

Thoughts become things.
-Mike Dooley

What we are today comes from our thoughts of yesterday, and our present thoughts build our life of tomorrow: Our life is the creation of our mind.
-Buddha

You are what you think, not what you think you are.
-Bruce MacLelland

Choose Your Words Wisely

If your intended outcome, your goal, is powerfully affected by how you see it in your mind before you even begin the process of creating it in the physical world, then it is important that you consider carefully how that picture appears. The way to ensure that you have the image of the outcome that you truly want when you achieve your goal is to choose the wording of your goal carefully.

Earlier, we discussed the difference between stating that you want to lose weight and stating what your intended outcome is. Stating your intended outcome is very powerful, as it gives your mind something crystal clear to focus on. This becomes the beacon for you to continuously move toward. You may have heard of the Law of Attraction. This law states that like attracts like and, essentially, that you create what you think about. There has been much written about the Law of Attraction, and just about as much criticism of it. Whatever your beliefs about the Law of Attraction, when not oversimplified into the notion that you can simply create anything solely by thinking about it, it is very important to frame your goals with positive language that allows your mind to focus clearly on exactly what you want.

Most people think in visuals, so once you have written down your goal, the language in it will trigger an image. If your goal is "lose weight," what picture will you get in your mind? Try to visualize that now. What do you actually see in your mind's eye? You may see yourself in your present overweight body, standing on a scale. You may see an image of someone with rolls of fat around their middle. You may see images of diet commercials from television. You may even notice a feeling of stress come over you if this has been a struggle in the past.

This is where the "like attracts like" concept comes in. If what you write down is "I want to lose weight," you begin to think about losing weight. If what you are thinking about is losing weight and that thought projects an image of being overweight into your mind, then you begin to feel the stress of the burden of losing weight, the shame and pain you have felt in the past about your body and the unsuccessful attempts at diets you have been on. The negative picture triggers a negative reaction in your mind. This is like attracting like. This is not a motivating place to be in to take action! You want to word your goals such that the image you create in your mind is undoubtedly positive and *exactly* what you want to create in the physical world.

Here are some examples of goals that have been written in ineffective language and transformed into effective language:

I want to quit smoking in one month

The goal is specific; it is measurable, achievable, certainly rewarding, possibly very risky and there is a timeline attached. Here is where the wording needs to be adjusted: The word *smoking* is in the goal. Every time you read this goal, what picture will you get in your head when you see this word? Perhaps you will see an image of a cigarette with a plume of smoke rising from it. Perhaps you will even see yourself actually taking a drag from a cigarette. Or maybe you will visualize yourself struggling and fighting with the cravings for a cigarette. What emotions will that trigger? How likely is it you will feel motivated *not* to smoke when you keep unintentionally visualizing smoking? Let's rephrase this into:

I will have powerful, clean, healthy lungs in 30 days

Now what do you see? Perhaps you see yourself walking up stairs without getting out of breath. Perhaps you see yourself breathing clean air. Or you may even see the clean, pink lungs in your chest, unencumbered by tar and pollutants. Which emotions do the phrase *powerful, clean, healthy lungs* trigger? How likely is that you will be motivated not to smoke when you visualize this image in your mind?

Any goal can be phrased in these terms. Here are some examples.

I want to quit my job and do something better

could become

I will spend the next 30 days exploring work that makes me feel purposeful and I will find the perfect career for myself

I want to get out of debt

could become

I will find creative solutions to manifest $7,000 of extra income into my life within the next 90 days

I want to be in a relationship

could become

I will be in a relationship with a wonderful man/woman, who is my perfect partner, in three months

I want to get in better shape

could become

I will be in great condition and run my first marathon in 90 days

The language in all of these reframed goals is positive, powerful and active. The language is reframed from what you *want* to what you *will have*. Want to be/have/do is a phrase that implies desire, which is fine, but it's not action. Will be/have/do is a phrase that implies intention to act. This may seem like a small shift but it is a powerful shift. Do not underestimate the power of your language. The more focused you are on exactly what you want, in as specific and vivid language as you can create, the better!

Look back on your goals. Take time now to reframe each of the goals you plan to work on using the tools in this chapter. Once you have done this, state the goal to yourself with your eyes closed. Pay attention to the image it conjures up in your mind. Realize your goal in your mind. Notice how you feel when you see yourself living in the world of that goal having been achieved.

Get Absolutely Crystal Clear

I cannot stress enough the power of having a clear goal. You must have it worded such that your outcome, once the goal is achieved, is absolutely crystal clear. Be sure you have used SMART language and chosen your words to be active by using the language that clarifies the intention of what you will create. In order to Realize your goal in the world, you have to Realize it in your mind by seeing a clear picture of your intended outcome. This means the result that you want. You can only do this by stating your goal as you intend to see it when it is achieved.

You may find yourself feeling some hesitation here, as there is one obstacle people often come up against when getting their crystal-clear goal in mind: "How am I going to do this?" The brain seems to want to figure out the mechanism of *how* before committing to the intention. This is why many people never take any action on their desires. Needing to know how you are going to do it before you commit is the exact opposite of what you need to do! Let go of needing to know how you are going to achieve your goals and simply get clear about your intended outcome. Remember the old adage, *necessity is the mother of all invention*? There are infinite "hows" available to you to support you in achieving your goals, but you will not discover them unless you get clear that you *will* create the outcome you desire. That clarity sets up the conditions for you to step out of your proverbial box, and begin trying things you would never have thought of before, in order to achieve your goal.

I remember when I first wrote down the goal of owning my own home. I resisted writing down the words,

I will have a signed purchase agreement for an investment property, with all subjects removed, on or before April 16th.

I did not want to write them down because the idea of how I was going to do this was overwhelming! And so if I wrote it down, I was going to have to figure out how I, already being in $20,000 plus of debt with no savings, was going to buy my first home in three very short months.

I convinced myself to write down this goal despite not having the faintest idea of how I would find a way to purchase a home. Even the process of writing it down caused my heart to pound. (I have since learned that this is a very good sign, as it implies that I am stepping out of my comfort zone, which is always when I grow the most.) So without any idea how I was going to accomplish it, I decided to let go of worrying about the how, and simply trusted that I would find a way. I did not need to know how right now. "How" was only going to get in the way of seeing the possibility of accomplishing it. I had to commit to the goal with a clear vision of my intended outcome so that I could then invent the way to create it. If I had to figure out how I was going to do it first, I would have never committed, because buying a home in three months whilst in debt, with no savings, really seemed impossible!

Stay out of the "how" trap. Write down your goal. Do not worry about how you will achieve it now. Trust that you will find the way, and you will. You may not see the "how" yet, but once you set a clear intention that you will achieve your goal, you will find a way.

Get that crystal-clear goal written down. **R**ealize it in your mind. Believe that a way exists (even if you have no idea what that is yet) for you to accomplish it because your intention is clear. Put your goal somewhere that you will see it every day (I like the door of the refrigerator). When you see your goal, focus on the outcome, not the obstacles. You will be amazed at the solutions that find their way to you when you trust the process. This is a huge step toward achieving your goal, as the creative process always starts by **R**ealizing it in your mind first.

Visualize

Visualizing is an incredibly powerful tool to help you **R**ealize your goal. And, indeed, it requires **R**ealizing it in your mind first in order to create it as a reality in the physical world. Visualizing is the process of imagining pictures of what you want to achieve in your mind. It is one of the simplest and easiest tools to use. You don't even have to get out of bed to visualize!

Human beings are visual creatures. If someone says the word *fire* and you close your eyes and consider what you see in your mind's eye, you will likely see the image of fire rather than the word *fire*. We dream in images, not in sentences and paragraphs. Images in our minds are powerful ways to focus our thoughts.

The power of visualization is well documented. Researchers Christopher Davoli and Richard Abrams studied the use of visualization techniques on performance of tasks and concluded that the mind is a very powerful tool. "[This is] an idea that has long been espoused by motivational speakers, sports psychologists, and John Lennon alike: The imagination has the extraordinary capacity to shape reality."

Stories and studies abound that attest to the power of visualization. A tennis player who is injured and cannot practice on the court visualizes the court in his mind for the same number of hours a day as he would have in the actual court and is able to return to 90 percent of the performance he had prior to being laid up. A prisoner in solitary confinement in the USSR for nine years played himself on a chessboard in his mind and, when released, was able to beat the world champion chess player in 1996. Celebrities, public speakers, authors and famous athletes such as Tiger Woods, Deepak Chopra, Oprah Winfrey, Anthony Robbins, Jack Nicklaus all attest to the incredible power of visualization to enhance their careers, improve their health and create their dream lives.

Research in cognitive and brain sciences explain that when we visualize something, the brain reacts exactly the same as if it is experienced it in reality. Based on this visualization, neural connections are created just as they would be if you were physically doing something.

Another explanation for why visualization works comes from psychologists who state that visualizations help reprogram automatic negative thought patterns to more positive ones, allowing people to take action that creates better results in their lives. More metaphysical explanations suggest that, in addition to scientific and psychological explanations, thoughts are energy frequencies. They also suggest that a clear, focused thought puts out an energy that will attract a situation, person or object into your life as an energetic frequency match to what you need. This is essentially the Law of Attraction.

Regardless of whatever explanation you believe (and I believe all of them), visualization works. I have used visualization and had uncanny results on many occasions. Hearing my father use the exact words that I heard over and over again in my visualizations of creating my dream job still gives me shivers.

At one point, I was going to have a conversation with my boss in which I was going to ask for something that I felt really uncomfortable asking for. I was motivated to ask because if she said yes, it would help me take a big step toward achieving a goal I had. For a few days before I had the conversation with her, I visualized sitting with her in her office and I visualized the conversation going exactly as I had hoped it would go. Each time I had this visualization, I saw her in a particular mustard-yellow suit. I don't know why she always arrived in my mind wearing that suit, but she did. In the course of my imagined conversation with her, she always said, "We would really like to help you out with this, Monica." And at the end of our meeting in my mind she shook my hand.

The day of the actual meeting, I arrived at her office, knocked on the door and, you guessed it, she was wearing the exact mustard-yellow suit I had seen her wear in my mind. At the end of our discussion, again, she used the exact words I had heard in my head, "We would really like to help you out with this, Monica."

I could go on and on with rather striking examples like this, but essentially what I now know and trust is that it works. This tool is at your disposal any time you shut your eyes. Play with it!

There are a few things that one can do to enhance the effectiveness of a visualization:

1. Start by getting comfortable and relaxed somewhere that you will not be disturbed for a few minutes. Settle yourself. Let go. Relax your body. Slow your breathing. See yourself walking on a beautiful path that leads you to your goal. This is not necessary in order to visualize, but may help you get used to the practice and enhance the experience, especially if you are new to it. (If visualizing comes easily to you, you can close your eyes for fifteen seconds at a stoplight and do a quick visualization!)

2. Visualize, as clearly as you can, the exact outcome you want to create. It is difficult to hold a static image in your mind, so try to see a scenario unfolding. It may help to see it on a screen, like in a cinema in your mind. You may watch yourself in your new circumstance or you may actually be experiencing your life out of your own eyes.

3. Involve as many senses as you can. Where are you? How vivid can you make the colours? What do you smell? What do you hear? Get detailed. Are people congratulating you on achieving your goal? What exactly are they saying to you? Are they shaking your hand? Feel the emotional response to your new circumstances. Enjoy it!

4. Repeat! But do not make this a chore. Visualizing should be a fun way to enjoy focusing on the amazing future you are creating! The more you do it, the more effective it will be.

Let's go back to the "quit smoking" goal from Chapter 1.

Goal: *I will have powerful, clean and healthy lungs in 30 days.*

Here is a possible visualization to match this:

In your mind, you see yourself walking on an uphill slope, possibly in an area you are already familiar with. You notice the details of where you are walking, the type and colour of the trees, the grasses growing by the side of the path. You can smell a freshness in the air. You note the temperature around you, perhaps it is autumn and the air is cool. You see yourself wearing a particular outfit. Maybe a new blue brand name tracksuit with two white stripes down the legs and a pair of new runners. You hear the crunch of gravel under your feet. You notice the pace you are walking and you feel the clean air going into your lungs. You notice how easy it is to breathe, how cool the air feels filling up your lungs. You feel great. You are keenly aware of the fact that, heading upwards on the incline, you feel no resistance in your lungs. Your breath begins to increase but you do not feel winded, you feel strong, fresh and powerful. Your throat is clear and the cool, clean air flows in and out of your clean, healthy lungs. You feel you could continue your hike forever. You feel amazing!

Notice the detail in this visualization. It includes the use of your physical senses: the fresh air smell, the coolness of the air entering your lungs, the sound of gravel under your feet, the appearance of the physical environment around you. It also includes you doing exactly what you wish to do, which is to be unencumbered by the physical effects of your smoking addiction without focusing on *not smoking* but rather focusing on the *results* that not smoking will give you. It is not a static image but one that uses movement so that you can hold the visualization more easily. The visualization has you focus on how great you feel as a result of what you have created. You are Realizing your goal in your mind. This will propel you to realize it in reality.

Vision Boards

Another powerful visualization-related tool that you can use is a vision board. A vision board is simply a large piece of poster board that you cover with images of the end results you want to create. You already have a very clear statement about the goals that you want to achieve. The vision board reinforces the Realizing of your goals in your mind. The vision board can make your intended outcome indelible in your mind.

Vision boards can be created in any way you wish. You can create a collage of many different images or pick a single one that you find very inspiring. You can make it very large or relatively small. You can have one vision board for each of your goals or you can put them all together. You can cut images out of magazines or take photos of what you want to create. You can draw or paint images of what you want. You can put a picture of yourself looking ecstatic because you have created all the things that are in the collage around you. You can put your stated goals in writing under the images that you have created. The idea is simply reinforcing the goal through a visual image that focuses your attention on it whenever you see it.

There is a very compelling story about the effects of a vision board in the movie version of *The Secret*. John

Assaraf describes moving into his dream house and, while unpacking, he finds a vision board that he had created several years before. When he looked at the images on the board, he was shocked to find that he had moved into the dream house that he had on his vision board. Not a house similar to the one in the image, but the exact house!

My own experience with vision boards has been similar. I recently pulled out a vision board that I created about four years before. I, too, was surprised to see on the vision board that I had pasted all kinds of images of volunteers abroad. I remembered back then that it was a dream to go to an African country and volunteer to make some kind of difference in the world. It was incredible to look at this image because I had forgotten that I had even made this vision board, but I had actually been selected along with five other teachers across Canada to work with the Jane Goodall Institute and Ugandan Ministry of Education as a volunteer to train teachers in environmental education in Uganda two years prior! On my vision board, one photograph was a of a woman in the country where she volunteered, with a quote above that said, "My time in Africa let me see my world from a new and thankful perspective." Above the photograph I had pasted the words *help the planet* and *earth-friendly*.

Vision boards, like visualization, focus your attention over and over again on what you want to create. But the power of vision boards (and visualization) to help you Realize your goal in your mind can be explained from a psychological perspective too. There is a system in your brain that filters information, called the reticular activating system. This is at the base of our brain stem and its job is to sort and evaluate incoming data. The reticular activating system tags stimuli as being important and, thus, directs your attention there. It can also tag information as unimportant and allow you to ignore it. This is an important function that allows you to focus on what you need to and tune out what you don't need to give your attention to. Can you imagine arriving on the Las Vegas strip and trying to find your way to a particular restaurant without your reticular activating system in place? You would not be able tune out any of the noise, lights and people! You would be overwhelmed with stimulation and might never arrive at your destination, never mind make it down to the end of the street!

The vision board can reprogram your reticular activating system to focus on events and things in your environment that support you in achieving your goal. It programs your mind to pay attention to things in your environment that align with your intended goal. You have likely noticed how the reticular activating system works when you decide that you want a particular new car. Once you have decided that you are going to buy that car, it seems that someone on every block is driving one! Of course, that car was just as abundant on the streets as the day before you decided you wanted one, but your reticular activating system had not yet tagged that make and model as important, so you simply were not seeing them. Now it is important to you, so your reticular activating system is tagging those cars as something to pay attention to.

So as you create your vision board, be sure to choose images and words that really resonate with the vision you have of your goal achieved. Every time you look at your vision board, you are reinforcing the importance of those images to your reticular activating system, so the more specific you can be, the more directly and accurately your brain can pick up and tag important information in your environment to draw your attention to.

Finally, the strategic placement of your vision board is very important. Place it somewhere that you will see it over and over again. Stop in front of it when you pass by. Spend a few minutes looking at the images and feel the feelings of passion and excitement that they elicit in you. If you find that your vision board is becoming wallpaper and you constantly pass by it without taking in what is there, then move it. Put your vision board in a new place where you will see it as fresh again. If looking at your vision board stops eliciting an emotional response from you, update it. Enhance or add images and words to bring back that feeling of excitement again.

The power of **R**ealizing your goal in your mind is clear. **R**ealize it in your mind first and you will Realize it in reality.

Summary

R is for **R**ealize It in Your Mind First in The D**R**EAM
Power Goal System

Before you create anything in the outside world, you create it in your mind. You must get clear on exactly what you plan to create and **R**ealize it in your mind first.

Choose Your Words Wisely

The language you use to word your goal has a direct impact on the vision of your achieved outcome in your mind. Choose your words wisely. Frame your outcome in the positive by stating what you want, not what you don't want. Use language that implies intention (I will) and not desire (I want). Ensure that when you state your goal to yourself, it conjures up an image of exactly what you intend to create as your result.

Get Absolutely Crystal Clear

State your goal so that you Realize in your mind exactly what you want your result to be. Let go of how you will create it. It is only by committing to the goal, despite not knowing the mechanism that you will use to achieve it, that your creative solutions can be stimulated.

Visualize

The mind sees in images, so Realize your goal in your mind by visualizing your intended outcome in your mind. Take some time to relax. Picture yourself, as vividly as you can, living your intended outcome of your goal. See it like a movie rather than a static image. Include your sensory perceptions in your visualization. Add as much detail as you can. Connect with the feelings of excitement, pleasure and pride in living your intended outcome. Visualize your goal achieved often, but do not make it into a chore.

Vision Boards

Visualization and vision boards reprogram your reticular activating system, by changing what this system draws your attention to. Create a vision board by making a collage or drawing images of your goal achieved. Add words that elicit strong positive emotions. Place the vision board strategically in your home and connect with the emotions that it elicits regularly. Change its location or update the images if they no longer stimulate you.

Now that you have **R**ealized your goal in your mind, learn how to **E**nergize and connect to your passion!

DREAM
Energize!

The more intensely we feel about an idea or a goal, the more assuredly the idea, buried deep in our subconscious, will direct us along the path to its fulfillment.

- Earl Nightingale

You know that how you are feeling can affect how you act. If you are in a good mood, you are far more likely to be effective at what you are doing. However, we rarely make a conscious decision to create our mood. Energize is all about using tools to create an Energized, emotionally exciting, invigorated, passionate state! When you are in this state, your energy shifts and you move toward your goals with enthusiasm! In this chapter, you will learn tools to get you into this Energized state.

Align With the Truth of Who You Are

The truth of who you are exists at your core. Beneath the layers of self-doubt, negative thoughts, worries and fears, you are a being who is capable of achieving anything. At your core, you are unconditionally loving and absolutely know that you are unconditionally loved. At your core, you are confident, curious and creative and you express yourself without fear so you are completely honest. At your core, you are not afraid to take risks, you are undeniably enthusiastic and you have a strong, intact sense of self-esteem. At your core, you are a success-breeding machine!

Now, you might be thinking that you do not exhibit many of these qualities on a daily basis, so how can you claim that is who you truly are? Think of a baby. Are there any of these qualities that a baby is not? What is possible for a baby? Essentially, anything is possible for a baby. Virtually all babies show these qualities for the first year or so of their lives. And just like those babies, you are born with these qualities. At your core, this is the truth of who you are.

So why doesn't every person go around living these qualities every day? The answer is because, as we grow, circumstances happen to us in our lives. And as a result, we cloud over our core with negative self-beliefs. Perhaps we are spoken to in a way that makes us feel worthless. Perhaps we are abused. Perhaps we are given messages from others about our social status. Perhaps we are bullied. Perhaps we watch our parents go through a divorce. Everyone lives through experiences that can be perceived as negative. We give meaning to those experiences. We subconsciously make decisions about ourselves when we experience these things. We think that because kids are bullying me and calling me names there must be something wrong with me. I must somehow be flawed. Subconsciously we begin to form beliefs about ourselves, such as we are not deserving, not lovable or not capable.

We begin to see more and more events in our lives as evidence of our not deserving, not being capable or whatever it is that we have decided about ourselves. These become automatic thought patterns that we are not even conscious of.

Once our automatic negative thought patterns have set neural pathways in our brain, our behaviours begin to change to match these beliefs and ultimately create results in our lives that we do not want. You likely know someone who constantly meets a new partner whom they are really excited about. This is the soul mate, the love of your friend's life. But within a short period of time, your friend finds that they are unhappy and complaining about exactly the same problems that they had with the last person they dated. It seems that they continue to recreate the same relationship over and over again with different people. It is not really the other people that are to blame for unhappy relationships, but the fact that somewhere that person has a self-belief about not truly deserving the relationship that they really want. So, instead, they subconsciously continuously create the circumstances to attract the same kind of unsatisfying relationship with each new partner.

We are not aware of the fact that we have these negative self-beliefs, and continually create self-fulfilling prophecies to prove ourselves right. And because all of this is going on in the subconscious level of our minds, we blame other people, and life, for our circumstances. We feel unhappy, anxious, powerless, resentful or simply numb.

Those feelings of unhappiness, anxiousness, powerlessness, resentment and numbness appear when our thoughts and actions do not line up with our core qualities. When we think and behave in ways that are not in alignment with who we truly are at our deepest core — that loving, confident, creative, honest inner self — we feel painful emotions. Negative emotional responses are incredibly valuable tools for knowing that you are not in alignment with who you *really* are. Your negative emotions are gifts to you. When you are feeling negative, simply notice it. Do not fight your negative feelings and do not numb them. Accept they are there, let them wash over you and even allow yourself to be grateful for them as they are telling you that you are out of alignment. Once you have spent a few minutes consciously experiencing your negative emotions, let them go. This is really important! Often we will wallow in our negative feelings about ourselves. We will use them as reasons to beat ourselves up, to excuse ourselves from action or to have a pity party.

Energize! is all about accessing your essence. When you Energize, you realign with who you really are. When you are connected to your core values, you feel aligned with your true self. This is exciting and empowering!

On some level, you know that are capable of whatever it is that you need to do to achieve your goals, even if it is hard to access that knowing right now. This knowledge allows you to take action. If you allow yourself to wallow in the beliefs that you have layered upon the truth of who you are, you will likely not succeed in achieving what you want.

The rest of this chapter has tools to Energize you. These tools allow you to connect to that truth of who you are: capable, unconditionally loved and loving, confident, curious, creative, honest, risk-taking, enthusiastic and deserving. I cannot overstate the importance of using the

Energize tools for goal achievement! Even if you just use these tools and nothing else, your life will change. When you put them together with the rest of the DREAM Power tools, you can achieve anything!

Emotionalize

Thoughts and Emotions

The first tool to Energize you is to inject your goals with positive emotions. This starts with how you think. Your thoughts affect your emotional state and your emotional state affects your behaviour. When you are feeling good, excited, happy, empowered and joyful, you will walk down the street with a little skip in your step. You will look people in the eye and smile at them. You might feel the sudden urge to pick up some flowers for someone you are seeing later, just because you know it will make them feel happy. This behaviour, in turn, makes you feel even better!

We have far more control over our emotions than we think we do. Most people believe that emotions are externally triggered. They are not; we just think they are because we spend most of our time on automatic pilot. You have tremendous power to affect your emotional state and doing so is a great way to put some energy behind the action you take to achieve your goal.

Many years ago when I lived in England, I was in a very serious relationship with an English man. Everything indicated that this relationship would be "the one." I had little doubt that we would get married and live happily ever after. A year or so into the relationship, I could sense something had changed but I had no idea what was wrong or why things were different. I began to worry constantly that something was very wrong and he would leave me. Sure enough, the man of my dreams ended our relationship. I was devastated. I did not fully understand what happened or why it was over but it was clearly over. I went through quite a deep grief for a while, as I had been very much in love. I felt a lot of pain. I was angry with him for hurting me and with myself for doing whatever it was that I had done to cause him to change how he felt about me. My heart would well up with feelings of sadness that he was gone. I would get distracted for short periods of time and then it would pop back into my head, reminding me it was over. I felt terribly sorry for myself. I was wallowing in misery, going from sad to angry to depressed to hopeless and then back to sad again. My poor pillow had been soaked with tears and then beaten senseless enough times that it looked how I felt: a sad, limp, deflated version of itself. I was struggling.

At the time that we had split, I was about to have a week off work, which I had planned to spend with him in Brighton. Since that was obviously not happening now, I was stuck in London on my own, without the distraction of my job in the middle of this grief. I decided that I would get myself out of the house every day for a walk. I liked central London and I usually ended up reading in a bookstore coffee shop overlooking the street below. Being the emotional wreck I was, I gravitated to the self-help section and, in one book that I picked up, I began to read about how my reaction to my circumstances was in my control. This book talked about how I could change my thoughts, which, in turn, would change my emotional reaction.

As I reprocessed my circumstances with this new insight, I felt a sudden freedom from the despair I was feeling. I began to consider the relationship in a different way. I had learned a tremendous amount from it. I had had the opportunity to experience a deep love of a kind I'd never experience before. And I was now learning a new approach to my emotions. I realized that all of these were things I could be happy about. I could be grateful for the opportunity to have loved and felt love. I felt happy that I had the chance to learn about relationships the way I had with this man. I was glad that I was sitting in this café every day reading about new ways to see the world. I actually felt *happy*. And even more surprisingly, because of what I was learning, I felt grateful that the breakup had happened!

Having said that, I would have jumped at the chance to go back with this man, had he offered. And if I smelled his cologne on someone on the Underground subway system, I still got a wave of sadness. But the lesson for me was that I could choose how to think about the breakup, and when I thought about it differently, the positive emotions I created felt empowering and energizing instead of agonizing and defeating. I felt ready to take on the world and see what great new experiences were ahead for me rather than live in the feelings of grief, anger and sadness of what I had lost in the past.

I do want to emphasize that I am not suggesting that, when perceivably negative emotions come up, we should not allow ourselves to experience them. I needed to grieve the loss of the relationship that I had believed would be the love of my life. It was very appropriate for me to feel sad for a period of time. The difference was that after an appropriate amount of grieving, I chose to think about the relationship from a different mind-set. I chose to focus on what I gained from having been in it, rather than what I lost. I chose to focus on being lucky to have had the opportunity to learn and love rather than to focus on the pain of rejection. When I made the choice to shift my focus, I created very positive emotions that empowered rather than weakened me.

Emotions are very, very powerful. Becoming conscious of the thoughts you choose to think and how they affect your emotional state on a day-to-day basis can change your life. You are in control of this. When big things happen, honour your emotional reaction and take the time to grieve. But on a day-to-day basis, you can choose to shift your focus to create a positive emotional response.

Instead of putting your attention on the jerk in the car that just cut you off and triggering an anger response, you can choose to consider that he is probably having a really bad day, is maybe late and is likely feeling quite unhappy. Then you may find you not only feel less angry but you may even be inclined to send him some love! It is simply a different choice of reaction.

Another reason to consider carefully your thoughts and resulting emotions is that every time you send out positive energy with your positive emotional state, you attract it back to you. And the same works in reverse.

Think about how you react to someone who is angry, bitter, cold, bored or simply just unhappy. Do you want to be around that person? Do you enjoy their company? Are you likely to smile at them? Are you likely to warmly engage them in conversation?

Now think about someone who is excited, happy, joyous or passionate. How do you feel when you are around a person like that? Do you feel better just being in their presence? Are you more likely to smile at them? React to them with warmth? What we put out comes back to us in this way. Our emotional energy attracts the same emotional energy back to us. Our emotional state can demotivate us or motivate us. Our emotional state can disempower us or Energize us. And it is our choice!

Propelling Your Goals Forward With Your Emotions

So how does this apply to our goals? You can propel the speed at which you achieve your goals by charging them with positive emotions. When you do this, you associate your positive feelings with your goal; you will feel Energized and ready to take on the world. In your mind, you have already begun visualizing what you want to create. When you visualize your outcome, *emotionalize* it. Fuel your vision with the positive emotions that you feel as a result of seeing your life with your intended goal achieved. As you see yourself at the door of your new boutique winery, with friends and family gathered around, smiling in anticipation, as you are about to officially open the door for business, how do you feel? Excited? Loved? Proud? As you visualize the event, feel the feelings that go along with it. This is your dream realized! You have done it! Let your heart well up with all the feelings that you have about this moment. Get totally into it! Energize yourself through your wonderful emotions!

If you have a hard time connecting with positive feelings when visualizing your goal, think back to a time when you have found success in your life. This can be anything that you feel good about. It can be as small as winning $20 in the lottery to as big as the birth of a child. Close your eyes and relive the feelings of those times. As you relive those past successes, awaken those feelings of happiness and exhilaration again and relish in them. Then, with this positive state of mind, begin visualizing your new goal accomplished. Connect that positive set of feelings from your past successes to the success of your imagined completed goal and again, relish it! Revel in it! Enjoy it!

When I do this, I generally choose a quiet place where I will not be disturbed because I can get so involved in my visualizations that I will be smiling, or even laughing out loud to myself. The more you get into the emotions of the visualization, the more powerful it is. When you are finished with your visualization, notice how you carry the emotional excitement with you into the world. You have focused your attention and energy on your positive feelings and now, as that energy stays with you, you step back into life and you are far more likely to take action on your goal. In this state, you are also far more likely to attract the right people to you to support you with what you need to achieve your goal.

When you think about your goal, do not allow yourself to spiral into thoughts of how challenging it is to take steps toward it; do not focus on obstacles or setbacks. Things will happen, sometimes you will feel frustrated, but this then becomes the most important time to think differently! Acknowledge your frustrations but do not wallow in them. If you try to deny or push away your frustrations, they will keep coming back. This can be as simple as admitting how you are feeling or it may require beating the stuffing out of your pillow, but once you have experienced what you need to, shift. Refocus, choose new thoughts and delight in the positive feelings you create!

This is an opportunity to have lots of fun because feeling good is fun! Test this out! As you positively emotionalize, pay attention to what happens. Notice people's reactions to you. See who comes along to help you with your goal.

Pay Attention to Coincidences

Coincidences can be very exciting if you pay attention to them because they can become indicators that you are on the right path. When a coincidence happens and it seems to fall into perfect alignment with what you are working on, this reinforces your choices and Energizes you!

Coincidence is defined in Wikipedia as "the noteworthy alignment of two or more events or circumstances without obvious causal connection." Many people take coincidences to be "flukes." However, you will find that if you begin to pay attention to them, coincidences are often actually better described as synchronicity (defined in Wikipedia as "the experience of two or more events, that are apparently causally unrelated or unlikely to occur together by chance, that are observed to occur together in a meaningful manner"). That is, when we pay attention to the coincidences of our lives, they can reinforce the path we are taking, they can guide us more quickly toward our outcome and, sometimes, they can help us take quantum leaps toward what we are trying to achieve.

Several years ago, I woke up one morning with a thought I could not seem to get rid of. It was about going on the Camino de Santiago, a walking pilgrimage, across northern Spain. This was something I had read about years before and always thought I would do but never really considered taking any real action toward. As I couldn't get this walking pilgrimage out of my head, I logged onto my computer and started reading about it. I read article after article about other people's journeys and I became very excited about taking this walking pilgrimage myself. I began to mentally sketch out a plan of when I could go.

Over the next few days, my excitement about the possibility of actually going on this pilgrimage began to grow. Then a series of coincidences began. At a dinner party, I mentioned the Camino de Santiago and one of the people at the party had been herself. This, in and of itself, may not seem like a great coincidence, but at the time only a few thousand people around the world went on the Camino annually, and most people had never heard of it. I became pretty excited when I heard she has been and she gave me some invaluable advice about footwear (the walk is about 25 kilometers a day for a month!)

I felt Energized by the coincidence and the ensuing conversation I had with the past pilgrim, and so I continued planning and researching the journey. A particular guidebook that I really wanted was repeatedly mentioned on websites, but I could not find a copy of it anywhere. I had tried all the main bookstores and was even unable to order it online.

Shortly thereafter, on a sunny afternoon, I took a wrong turn on my way home from an outing, and realized that I was on a street where there was an independent bookstore that I had been to years before. The bookstore was another ten minutes or so down the street but I figured that as I was already off course for heading home, it couldn't do any harm to pop in.

When I arrived, there was a single empty parking spot right outside the store. I parked, noting that the spot seemed to be reserved for me, walked in and wandered down an aisle somewhere in the middle of the shop. In that first aisle, I turned and faced the shelves of books and that is when I became very excited: All the books were spine out except for one. Yes, as unbelievable as it sounds, the only book that had its cover, rather than its spine, facing out and directly in my line of vision, was the book I was looking for. I remember standing there with my mouth hanging open, thinking somehow this was a trick! That someone had set it up so that I would find this particular book, which I had been searching for, staring me in the face, after an unplanned journey to the bookstore, because I took a wrong turn! This series of coincidences energized me to the point where I was almost bubbling over with excitement at the cashiers counter. I was so excited that I infected the clerk with my enthusiasm and he was laughing by the time I finished my transaction!

I could have chosen to call this a fluke or just a coincidence but, instead, I chose to assign a meaning to this. It affirmed for me that this journey was one I was supposed to go on. I felt very excited by this book being presented to me in such an unexpected way! I was invigorated and energized and began to take the next steps in planning the trip.

As I have mentioned before, money had always been an issue for me. The Camino de Santiago literally translates to "the road" or "path of Saint James". It is a pilgrimage from the French side of the Pyrenees to Santiago de Compostela in northwestern Spain. People have trekked it since before the time of Christ and later it became very popular as a pilgrimage to the relics of Saint James, held in a cathedral in Santiago de Compostela. For the last few hundred years, people had stopped following the pilgrimage but over the last twenty or so years, its popularity as a Christian, spiritual, reflective or physically challenging pilgrimage has increased again. In order to do this pilgrimage, one must have a few hundred dollars' worth of gear (backpack, shoes, rainwear, etc.) and, of course, money for a flight, food and *albergues* (pilgrims' hostels).

I had calculated the cost of this journey and simply did not have any money to pay for it. I had also been working in England for several years and had quit my job there to return to Canada. As I had been paying into retirement plans whilst living there, and was suddenly leaving the country permanently, I received a totally unexpected reimbursement cheque for the plans that I had paid into. The cheque was for enough money to cover the entire cost of the trip, almost to the dollar. Here was another coincidence that I could look at as a bit of luck or assign a bigger meaning to. I chose to assign a bigger meaning to it and, Energized by this indicator that I was on the right path, I booked the trip immediately!

That trip was one of the most significant experiences of my life. My development as a person took a quantum leap on that Camino de Santiago. What I learned there could fill another book, but what I learned about paying attention to coincidences and how I chose to view them has been a tool that has energized and guided me ever since. When I think of the coincidences that occurred, they were like synchronistic events that aligned to affirm my choices, to excite me and to allow me to get to where I wanted to go (literally and figuratively) much more quickly.

Coincidences can be written off and ignored or given attention and meaning. It is your choice.

Coincidences can also be looked at in another way. When you get clear about what it is that you want to achieve, and you are focused, excited and beginning to take action, coincidences may begin to show up that reinforce your path. Coincidences can be perceived as a form of the Law of Attraction. That is, when you are clear about your goal, you believe that you will achieve it and you set up positive thought patterns and emotions around it. Circumstances that match your internal mind space seem to appear to support you in creating what you want. Whatever you choose to believe about coincidences is up to you. I simply challenge you to pay attention to them and use them as a tool to Energize you on the path to your goal!

Give It Away

Think of your goal. What is it that you want to achieve? This is something that you really, really want for yourself. Now, give it away.

Huh?

Yes, give it away!

When you are about to launch into the process of creating your goals, get yourself psyched up by doing something that scares you just a little bit. You can do this by letting go of something you are holding onto tightly and giving it to someone else. This may be a risk for you either because it is frightening to let it go or because it is frightening to connect enough with another to give it away. But risking in order to give can be incredibly Energizing!

If you want an amazing relationship with someone (be it family or romantic), give away love as unconditionally as you can, as often as you can: volunteer somewhere where people feel lost or lonely, offer someone struggling with bags some help, really listen to someone you care about express their pain, smile warmly at a stranger. Notice how it Energizes you.

If you want to increase your sales, help someone else increase theirs with no expectation of return: give them a lead that is not quite right for you, share a sales technique that has been very useful to you, give credit to a coworker who deserves it. Notice how it Energizes you.

If you want your new business to be successful, be genuinely happy for someone else's success: send a card or a gift basket congratulating them, patronize their business and revel in their success, offer them support if you have a skill that is useful to them so that their business can continue to grow. Notice how it Energizes you.

If you want to lose weight, unconditionally support someone else in their goal, without expecting them to do the same for you. Notice how it Energizes you.

If you have a financial goal, give away some money or objects of financial value. Getting the idea?

Scarcity Thinking

Most people live in scarcity thinking. This is a subconscious drive to get yours before someone else gets it—and once you have it, to hold on tight! Somehow we have been trained to believe, on some level, that there is only so much out there and when someone else gets some, there is less left for you. This thinking comes from fear, an emotion that is disempowering and anxiety provoking.

I can't tell you how many times girlfriends have told me of their own devastation over an ex-partner finding new love. There are so many wonderful people out there in the world but these women want to hold on to what they had with someone with whom the relationship has died. Again, this is the fear that there is not enough to go around. This kind of thinking stunts growth and keeps us closed.

When I have been single, I can confess to this same scarcity thinking when another girlfriend falls in love and starts a relationship, and I notice a little creeping feeling inside of disappointment! Why wouldn't I be happy for a friend who found love? Because I was caught in the thinking that there is only so much love to go around and someone I know has taken a little bit for herself, leaving a little less available for me. This always left me fearful and unhappy.

You have likely seen this kind of scarcity thinking in business. People who think in terms of scarcity hoard their clients, hide their strategies for work success, hesitate to give credit to others, believe they should have the biggest part of a profit and do not feel happy when others in their work place are successful.

Scarcity thinking can be impervious—people can even have scarcity thinking around time. We have all muttered, "I don't have time for that (or you) right now." And it might well be true. But holding on to time and not giving the quality of time shared with a loved one, or dedicated to a meaningful project because we are too busy, is also scarcity thinking. Scarcity thinking in time is very ineffective when it comes to goal achievement!

Scarcity thinking is focused on what we don't have, what we see as lacking, what we don't want to create, what we might lose. This comes from fear that there is not enough to go around, causing the need to hoard. That fear makes us hold on to what we have so tightly that we can no longer attract more. We save the "little" time, love, money, stuff, etc. for ourselves because we fear that if we share it we will not be able to get more. We end up living with anxiety of losing what we have and being fearful of others trying to take it from us. We become closed.

Abundance Thinking

Happiness is directly related to unconditional giving. Giving unconditionally can only come from a belief in the abundance of life. When you give away what you want to have for yourself, you are focusing on the belief that there is more than enough for everyone. This thinking fosters appreciation for what we already have. It is seated in trust, love and possibility. It suggests a belief and confidence that you can continue to create for yourself whatever you desire. It inspires creativity and win-win thinking. When you begin to practice giving and you begin letting go of the attachment to having it only for yourself, you will begin to see the amount of space you have to attract all that you have been asking for open up.

Scarcity thinkers feel they must hoard and hide. They often speak negatively and report less happiness. Abundance thinkers feel that life offers more than enough to go around and that they can give without fear. Abundance thinkers report high rates of inner security, confidence and happiness. Which one do you think is going to support you best in achieving your goals? Abundance thinking will Energize you!

So give away what you want. Of course, you need to be responsible and thoughtful when you do so! And, also, you must give from the heart, because you genuinely want to support someone, simply to see them happier than they were before you gave to them, not because you want something in return. Ten dollars given away, truly unconditionally, is far more effective than a hundred given to impress someone or because you think you will get something back for it. When you give willingly and freely, you are sending the message out that you believe there is more than enough and you shift your energy to one of abundance!

Give it away—whatever it is—and notice that giving and receiving become the same thing. Every time you give unconditionally, you will notice not only your shift to abundance thinking, but that you will also feel good. It may be subtle, or it may be profound, but your energy will lift and you will feel more positive, more loving and more happy. You receive when you give unconditionally.

Begin to practice this. Consider your goals right now. What can you give away that will directly, or indirectly, support the success of your goals? Notice how you feel when you give. Energize yourself through unconditional giving!

I am not religious but I wanted to include the following prayer from Mother Theresa because, to me, it inspires truly unconditional giving.

The Final Analysis

People are often unreasonable, irrational, and self-centered. Forgive them anyway.

If you are kind, people may accuse you of selfish, ulterior motives. Be kind anyway.

If you are successful, you will win some unfaithful friends and some genuine enemies. Succeed anyway.

If you are honest and sincere people may deceive you. Be honest and sincere anyway.

What you spend years creating, others could destroy overnight. Create anyway.

If you find serenity and happiness, some may be jealous. Be happy anyway.

The good you do today, will often be forgotten. Do good anyway.

Give the best you have, and it will never be enough. Give your best anyway.

In the final analysis, it is between you and God. It was never between you and them anyway.

Be Grateful

If the only prayer you said in your whole life was "thank you," that would suffice.
-Meister Ekhart

Gratitude is a wonderful way to shift our attention to the abundance of life. We have so much. There is simply so much available to us and we are incredibly fortunate to live in our part of the world. Yet we often focus on what is missing and what we don't like.

Being grateful focuses you on what you *do* have, what *is* working in your life and what abundance already exists for you. Being grateful allows you to notice that your life is actually pretty great already. When you focus on the things you have to be grateful for, it is very hard to complain about those little day-to-day frustrations. Gratitude for everything that you already have is a very, very powerful tool to Energize you!

When you are in a state of gratitude, you feel good. When you feel good, life seems easier, people are more receptive to you and you can be more outwardly focused. This in turn Energizes you more!

Gratitude is a form of love. Every time you express true gratitude, you are energetically emitting love. When you are grateful to someone, you are loving them. This is important: the more you give thanks, the more you give love. Ironically, showing gratitude makes you feel fantastic! That is to say, in the act of giving gratitude and love, *you* feel love whether those to whom you offer it do or not!

You can appreciate anything with feelings of gratitude. Gratitude does not just have to be for what you have. You can feel grateful for the love you feel when you think of your child. You can be grateful for the wisdom you carry. You can feel grateful for an opportunity you were given. And, of course, you can feel grateful for all the material things you have. When you feel truly grateful, and your heart is filled with the love and appreciation for what you have, you simply attract more of it to yourself.

Whatever we think about, and thank about, we bring about.
- Dr. John F. Demartini

As you begin your practice of gratitude, you may want to try some of the following to get into the habit of being grateful:

Gratitude Meditation: A powerful habit to develop is to take a few minutes of every day and silently go through what you are grateful for. You can do this as a quiet meditation before bed, you can do this as a traditional prayer ritual or you can simply spend the time you are in the shower going through as many things you can think of that you are grateful for.

Say Thank You: We say thank you often throughout the day. Saying thank you is a graceful and polite habit to have; however, when you are saying thank you habitually, you are not often really present and focused on the gratitude you feel for the action that someone has taken for your sake. You say thank you perhaps dozens of times a day already. Begin to practice saying thank you with a conscious consideration of what you are saying. Mean it. Look the person in the eye. People feel the difference between a habitual thank you and a consciously spoken thank you.

Through this process, you may become aware of people that you have not thanked and whom you want to thank because they bring a lot to your life. Say thank you to them without a specific reason. Call someone up and tell them how grateful you are to simply have them in your life. Send a thank you card to someone who is not expecting it but for whom you are grateful.

Gratitude Journals: Some people spend a few minutes every day writing down things they are grateful for. Writing things down can be especially useful if you are someone whose mind tends to wander easily. This allows you to focus clearly on what you are grateful for by sitting down and spending a few minutes writing it out. Gratitude journals are also nice to have because when you are not feeling like you are in a good space, you can look back on your gratitude journal and read through all the things you have that you are grateful for.

Gratitude for Challenges: If you think back on times when you have come across challenges, difficult circumstances or disappointments, you will find there was often a silver lining to those dark clouds. Sometimes that silver lining was a powerful period of growth. Sometimes the opportunity lost created a new, even better, opportunity that you would never have been presented with had the original opportunity not gone wrong. Sometimes the greatest disappointment leads to the most amazing change in your life. Remember the times that you have found that to be true and be grateful for the dark cloud because of the silver lining that it gave you.

A Word of Caution

Language is still important, even in gratitude. Often when feeling down, we are tempted to go through a list of things to be grateful for with the "at least" focus. "At least I have my health" is a lot less energizing and powerful than "I am so grateful that I have good health." That difference is significant and it will have an effect on how well gratitude works for you. Be truly grateful! Let it fill up your heart. Let gratitude wash over you as you think of all of the things you are grateful for. Go throughout your day thinking thoughts of gratitude. Be grateful for a good night's sleep. Be grateful for the fact that you have a fast, safe and convenient mode of transportation available to you to get to work. Be grateful for the cashier at your coffee shop who smiled kindly to you. Be grateful for the coffee itself!

Summary

E is for Energize in The DREAM Power Goal System

Energy is everything. Supercharge your goals with positive emotions and Energize yourself to propel to your finish line faster than you imagined possible!

Align With the Truth of Who You Really Are

At our cores, we are wellsprings of confidence, love, trust and *joie de vivre*. But as a result of emotionally painful experiences, we subconsciously make decisions about ourselves to explain why these events have happened. These beliefs are directly tied to our worthiness, sense of capability and lack of belief in how lovable we are. As life goes on, we behave in ways such as to prove the negative beliefs we have created about ourselves are true. These beliefs that we have created about ourselves cause us to feel anxious, powerless and depressed, along with a plethora of other painful emotions. When we are in alignment with the truth of who we are at our essence, we feel excited, empowered, invigorated, peaceful and Energized! The tools in the rest of this chapter allow you to Energize and connect with your essence and align with the truth of who you are: a capable, loved and deserving person.

Emotionalize

Emotions affect our behaviour as well as what we attract. Positive emotions excite and Energize us. While events in life can cause sad or painful emotions (and at times we must allow ourselves to feel these kinds of emotions), on a day-to-day basis how we choose to think evokes either positive or emotional reactions. Thus we are in far more control of our emotions than we think we are. We can use this. When you think about and visualize your goal, emotionalize it! Think thoughts of your goal achieved that excite you. Feel the pleasure, joy, pride and excitement of the goal achieved. Do this as often as you can!

Pay Attention to Coincidences

Coincidence can be seen as flukes or indications that you are on the right path. When you start noticing coincidences, they can be very Energizing because they can begin to seem like the universe is handing you clues, encouragement and reinforcement that you are on the right path. When you become clear and single minded in your focus on your goal, coincidences begin to show up everywhere. You can choose to see these as gifts sent to you to guide you on your way.

Give It Away

Give away what you want. If you want love, give it away. If you want money, give it away. Do so unconditionally. Giving away what you want may seem counterintuitive, but when you let go of the need to hold on tightly to what you have, and trust that there is more than enough for you to have more if you need it, you shift your energy from that of scarcity to abundance. This allows room for more to flow through and it also allows for creativity to develop. Giving feels great. When you give unconditionally, it is always returned to you. What is your goal? Find a way to unconditionally give away what you are seeking.

Be Grateful

Gratitude focuses us on abundance rather than lack. When you feel genuine gratitude you feel Energized about how wonderful life is! There is a profusion of ways to practice gratitude. Journal, pray or simply say heartfelt thank yous for all that you have. Feel how Energizing the joy of gratitude is.

Use these tools to Energize your spirit and connect to your essence and watch how quickly you begin to advance toward your goals! Now learn how to take powerful Action.

DREAM
Action!

The First Step

*A journey of a thousand miles begins with a single
step.*
-Lao-tzu

The above quote is very, very old but has been used
over and over again. That is because there is tremendous
wisdom in it: We must act. We must move. We may not
have the route all figured out, and a thousand miles is a
long journey, but we only need take one step at a time. It
is not possible to do anything except by doing it one step
at a time!

We often get overwhelmed at how we are going to do
everything that we think we need to do to get where we
want to go. This can seem extremely difficult when we
consider how far away the end goal appears to be.

Just take the first step. Start the journey. Worry about
one step at a time. Now that you have crystallized your
goals in powerful and motivating language, and you have
Realized them as completed in your mind, you *must* take

action. Part of the reason why there has been so much criticism around the Law of Attraction is due to the fact that some people have taken it to mean that one only has to think about what one wants and it will magically appear. This is not true. Having a clear intended outcome is an absolute necessity but it does not happen without action.

Taking the first step is where many people fall down. They come up with a bunch of reasons why now is not the right time to take the first step. Do any of these sound familiar?

It is not really the right time. When the kids' soccer season is over, I will have more time to focus on this.

There is never a perfect time. There will always be a reason why another time is better. Now is all you have.

My wife (husband, mother, father, son, daughter) is not supportive of what I want. I need to get them on board before I move forward.

Someone will always oppose you. This is their agenda and it is normal for those who love you to fear the changes you plan to make because it may affect them. There is no better way for you to get people on your side than to live your dreams and model your truth. And those who continue to oppose you would not have been won over to begin with. Allowing someone else's agenda to stop you from doing what you truly believe you want breeds pain and resentment. Trust yourself. Take the first step. You will find a way to deal with those in your life who do not offer support the way you want it to look.

I need to research or acquire some skills before I can take the first step.

No you don't. Doing is your teacher. Analyzing or researching a situation is often paralyzing. You can spend all of your time figuring out what you need to figure out in order to get started. Take action now. As you come up against what you need to learn, you will learn it.

When I began this book, I had no idea how to put together a book in a form that was publishable. I had no idea if I had the skill to write effectively for an audience. I was tempted to start taking writing classes and reading books for authors. But, I knew if I did that, I would not end up writing. I would end up spending all my time getting ready to write! Instead, I began to write. Did I come up against things that I needed to learn? Absolutely. I started by writing fiction and, as I wrote, I talked to writers and publishers and continued the process, I realized that I wanted to reformat what I was doing to truly move toward my greater vision, my dream of inspiring and supporting people in achieving their highest good. I learned through the experience of the process, not by becoming an expert before I started. I could have spent a year taking classes and learning how to become a good fiction writer, only to discover that I really wanted to write non-fiction once I got started. Instead, I jumped in with both feet and took action on the goal — and wrote this book in ninety days!

Take Action. Put your first footprint onto the path once you begin to move, and you will be amazed by what begins to unfold to support you on your journey.

Planned Action

You can use all the tools presented thus far in this book, but without Action, it is highly unlikely that you will achieve your goal. Having planned Action helps structure how you will work toward your goal. It also helps you prioritize, reduces procrastination and keeps you accountable to yourself. As you set out planned action steps and check them off when you complete them, you feel excited and proud of your efforts and Action toward your goal, which has a snowball effect and motivates you to move to the next step!

Plan your action steps using the following DREAM Power Goal System Action template, which is downloadable on the DREAM Power Goal System website.

Start by breaking your goal down into three manageable chunks. If you are working on a ninety-day goal, where would you need to be after thirty days? After sixty days? And, of course, you have already been visualizing where you will be after ninety days! Breaking your goal into smaller, easily manageable steps allows you to feel less overwhelmed by the idea of taking on the entire goal at the beginning.

Here is an example of how to set up the DREAM Power Goal System Action template.

Goal #1 To have $10,000 of extra income in a savings account on or before September 1st

Step 1: $3,500 on or before July 1st

Week	Monday Action	Yes ?	Wednesday Action	Yes ?	Friday Action	Yes ?
1	Plan Proposal for Extra Client		Deliver Proposal		Follow Up and Close	
2						
3						
4						

July 1ˢᵗ Congratulations! Step 1 is Complete. I have $3 500 in the Bank!

Step 2: $7,000 on or before August 1st

Week	Monday Action	Yes ?	Wednesday Action	Yes ?	Friday Action	Yes ?
1						
2						
3						
4						

August 1ˢᵗ Congratulations! Step 1 is Complete. I have $7 000 in the Bank!

Step 3: $10,000 on or before September 1st

	Monday Action	Yes ?	Wednesday Action	Yes ?	Friday Action	Yes ?
1						
2						
3						
4						

Congratulations! I am so happy and grateful now that I have $10,000 of extra income in a savings account on or before September 1st

As you can see, the DREAM Power Goal System Action template has the goal stated at the top and then broken into three steps, each of which are set to be achieved after thirty days. There is space for action to be decided and written down three times a week.

You will notice that the action has only been written in for Week 1. It is important to fill in the action steps as you go. You do not know what circumstances will begin to change and present themselves to you as you work on your goals. You will also find that you will become more creative as you take steps toward your goals, and you may be doing things in your second month that you would never have dreamed of doing in your first week.

As you take your action steps, check them off under the Yes? column. Look at it each day as you plan your next action steps. The DREAM Power Goal System Action template will keep you on course toward your goal. If you have good support around you, have someone hold you accountable to what steps you state you will take. Support and accountability will be addressed further in Chapter 5: Maintain Your Momentum.

As you go through your DREAM Power Goal System Action template, be careful to choose action that sets you up for success. You know the difference between realistic action and unrealistic action. Also be aware of not continuing to take the same action over and over again if it is not really moving you toward your goal. If you have tried something a few times and it is not as successful as you would like, do something different!

Just Do It

Procrastination is attitude's natural assassin. There is nothing so fatiguing as an uncompleted task.
-William James

Procrastination is truly a challenge for just about everyone. There have been countless times that I have known that the most important task I need to get done is looming over my head and I will do just about anything to avoid doing what I need to do. The list of excuses for not doing that task can be virtually endless. I will write a "to do" list and then prioritize the list. Have you noticed that, often, the most important task seems to be the least desirable task? Before I get started, there is a thought process that begins in my mind and it goes something like this: I should probably just tidy up, make a bite to eat, clean out the fridge, do the dishes, do the laundry, clean out under the bathroom sink, return those library books, do some yoga, call my father, call my brother, call my sister-in-law, call a friend in England I haven't spoken to in years, bake a cake and make a cup of tea and then I will get to the list. Often this list of avoidance tasks whittles away at my available time. By the evening I have given up on even getting to the main list. Instead, I will justify my inaction by telling myself that I have tomorrow and I will get up bright and early and get right onto the most important thing.

Until tomorrow. That is when I will lie in bed, talking myself out of getting up bright and early, telling myself that I deserve to sleep in. Eventually, I will get up, I will look again at the to do list and convince myself that doing a quicker, easier task on the list will get me motivated to do the most important task on the list. But, often, doing a less important task will lead me to believing that I deserve some sort of break and I will find myself at the end of the this day with a reorganized closet, a pot of vegetarian chili and the to do list, still there, uncompleted and staring me in the face.

Naturally, this leads me to guilt. Guilt is uncomfortable so I avoid it by distracting myself from it through perhaps food, a glass of wine, a social event or watching some sort of mindless reality TV. The consequence of watching B celebrities try to make a comeback by competitively dancing without training is that I will be awake at three in the morning worrying about what I should have done but did not do!

This cycle of procrastination is painful and energy zapping. It elicits feelings of guilt and avoidance. It is demotivating. Creating all those avoidance excuses requires energy. Feeling guilt requires energy. Carrying the burden of what we must do requires energy. Procrastination is a massively demotivating energy suck. However, it can be overcome.

Firstly, you must become conscious of your procrastination behaviour and be clear that it is not serving you. Secondly, once you know that you have something important to do, just do it.

Nike knew what they were doing when they created their "Just Do It" campaign. "Just do it" implies action without excuses. It is an empowering statement. If you know you have something important to do and before you began any avoidance or procrastination you just did it, right away, how would you feel? The hardest, most uncomfortable thing is done and over with. You are not carrying around the burden of the thought that you have this thing to do later. It is done! Would you feel lighter? Would you feel more energized? Would you be more likely to get onto the next task? Absolutely.

Get up. Choose the thing that you consciously know you would most like to avoid and get it done and out of the way! Feel good about your **Action** and ride those positive feelings to keep taking **Action** on your goals! Just do it.

Program Your Mind

Our subconscious minds have no sense of humor, play no jokes and cannot tell the difference between reality and an imagined thought or image. What we continually think about eventually will manifest in our lives.
-Robert Collier

As you take **Action**, continue to apply the other steps and tools in the DREAM Power Goal System. Programing our subconscious mind allows us to combine many of these tools *while* we are taking **Action**. This is exceptionally effective to propelling you forward.

The subconscious mind is the part of our mind that controls bodily functions, allowing us not to have to make conscious decisions such as to breathe each breath. The subconscious mind is also responsible for recording all events that have happened to us and our emotional *reactions to them.* Many of our habitual responses come from those beliefs that are buried within our subconscious mind (discussed in Chapter 3: Energize). As we learned, we often reinforce our own subconscious beliefs by thinking thoughts and taking action that strengthen what we already believe subconsciously about ourselves. In fact, subconsciously, we want to do this because our current thoughts and beliefs are comfortable and make us feel safe and in control.

The gift of the subconscious is that it is like the soil of a garden. It will grow whatever is planted there, if the garden is cared for. The beliefs that exist in our gardens today have been well cultivated and are very strong. We nurture those beliefs by focusing on them, looking for evidence that they are true, and simply by thinking about them over and over again. However, the subconscious can have new seeds — that is, beliefs — planted in it at any time. We then just need to nurture those seeds, our new beliefs, by focusing on them, looking for evidence that they are true and thinking about them over and over again.

The subconscious mind is neutral. It accepts what is impressed upon it, negative or positive, true or false, real or imagined. Your subconscious mind does not debate with you. It accepts your thoughts as you think them. The keys to impressing something on your subconscious mind are based on how emotionally charged your thoughts are and how often you think those emotionally charged thoughts. Knowing that you choose what you think about: understand how incredibly powerful this is!

So how do you use the subconscious mind to achieve your goals? You plant new seeds. Make a statement about what you plan to achieve as if you already have it. For example:

I am so happy, grateful and thankful now that I have a signed purchase agreement for an investment property on or before April 16th.

I referred to this goal in Chapter 2: **R**ealize. I used this statement over and over again to program my subconscious and, as you know, I achieved this goal in ninety days despite rather remarkable obstacles being in my way!

Here are the secrets to making these kinds of subconscious mind-programing statements more effective.

1. Faking It

Your statement is not true. Yet. Say it anyway. Remember, the subconscious mind does not know the difference between what is real and what is imagined. I had a very hard time believing that my statement would become true in ninety days as I did not have a penny to put toward a down payment when I first wrote that, and I could not begin to see how I was going to create it. In fact, I found it quite difficult to even say it in my head because, at first, I thought I was lying to myself. I trusted this technique enough to do it anyway and, little by little, I began to believe that it was possible. Ultimately, I had my signed purchase agreement in my hands on April 14th!

2. Repetition

Any belief is simply a thought that is repeated over and over again until it is taken as a reality. Repeat your statement to yourself as often as you think of it. Stick it up on sticky notes at strategic places around your house, in your car, at your office and anywhere else where you will be prompted to say it. As I repeated my statement to myself, over and over again, I began to see it as a possibility. Then, over time, it simply became crystal clear that I would create it.

3. Visualizing and Emotionalizing

You have learned the power of this in Chapter 2: Realize and Chapter 3: Emotionalize. Your subconscious mind responds to strong emotions, either positive or negative. Charge your statement with positive feelings. Use your visualizations of your completed goal and get those excited, energizing emotions aroused as you state your goal over and over to yourself. If you are having a hard time with connecting to the feelings you will feel when you have achieved your goal, here is one very powerful tool you can use to get excited again: Jump up and down and shout your statement aloud to yourself! If you are worried about being heard, drive somewhere where you won't be and shout it out!

You can also just challenge your self-consciousness and allow yourself to be heard declaring your goal with excitement in public. This will create an even bigger energy. I myself went downtown with a friend to a very busy street in Vancouver and shouted out an affirming statement in public as my friend video recorded me. I was giddy for the rest of the day! I then posted the video of myself on a social networking site and continued to ride the energy of the positive comments received from other people who watched my video! This amplifies the energy because you are not only sending out your own positive excitement about your goal but you are affecting other people with your positive energy and they, in turn, reflect that back to you.

One woman who practiced this technique went every morning for ninety days into a local shop and shouted her affirming statement three times at the entrance. No one ever said anything to her and she got a lot of odd looks. She felt embarrassed but did it anyway. One day, after the ninety days were up and she no longer came to jump and shout, she was in the store to pick up some milk. The cashier told her that she was so inspired by having seen this woman for the last three months, boldly stating her intended outcome of her goal, that she herself had decided to apply to university and had just been accepted into a course that she had previously felt unworthy of taking!

4. Present Tense

Notice that I stated my affirming thought in the present tense. The subconscious mind does not know reality from imagination so as I plant this seed, and consciously water and care for it with the other tools presented here, my subconscious mind begins to place my actions and behaviours so that they line up with the subconscious belief that this is already a reality.

5. Be Grateful

The benefits to being grateful have already been stated in Chapter 2, but you simply must not underestimate the power of gratitude. *Always start your affirming statement with "I am so happy and grateful now that I am/have ..."* and then connect to those same feelings of gratitude that you know you will have when what you are stating has become true!

6. Programing Before Bed

Sleep is our subconscious mind's playground. During sleep, we are given the opportunity to process the day. But what we think about before we go to bed is often what our subconscious mind gets to work on. Surely you have noticed that, as you fall asleep, if you are worrying about work, the kids or even a conversation that you had that was upsetting that day, you will dream (or perhaps have nightmares) about it. You also may not sleep well and you will often wake feeling less rested and anxious.

Before you go to bed, you have the opportunity to decide what thoughts will get steeped in the subconscious mind. Start with gratitude. Thank yourself for what steps (even if they were tiny) that you took toward your goal. Repeat your affirming statement to yourself while you visualize your life with your goal achieved. Ask your subconscious to help you work on solutions to obstacles that you may feel are in your way. Allow yourself to fall asleep filled with positive thoughts toward your goal.

When I began practicing this regularly, not only did I often wake up with new, creative solutions to obstacles that were in my way, but I began to be woken up by my own laughter! My dreams were literally so joyful that I would be laughing in my sleep loudly enough to wake myself up!

Summary

A is for **A**ction in The DREAM Power Goal System

Action is simply doing something that moves you closer to your goal. Planned or unplanned, take **A**ction!

The First Step

The first step is often the hardest step. It is easy to come up with reasons why you are not ready to actually take action. The temptation to get all the ducks lined up before making a move can hinder or even prevent you from ever getting started. Get yourself on the path. Take the first step.

Planned Action

Planned Action keeps you on course toward your goal. The DREAM Power Goal System Action template is an excellent way to structure each action step you take and track your progress.

Just Do It

We all succumb to times where endless excuses allow us to justify inaction. Connect to the potential of living from "just doing it" before you allow yourself to come up with excuses. Get the challenging tasks out of the way to start with!

Program Your Mind

Combine all of the chapters' tools to create positive, compelling statements about your achieved goal in the present tense. Use these statements to plant new seeds in your subconscious mind and reinforce them by stating them repeatedly, just as you would water and tend to a new seedling. This will galvanize the Action you are taking!

Now that you are on a roll, the next chapter will teach you how to Maintain Your Momentum.

DREAM
Maintain Your Momentum

You have come a long way! You have put the DREAM Power Goal System into effect. You have Decided on what you want. You have refined it to the point where you are crystal clear on the outcome you want to create. You are using the Realize and Energize tools and techniques on a daily basis—visualizing, being grateful, affirming your success—and you are planning and taking Action steps toward your goals. Continue following these steps in the DREAM Power Goal System and you will create the results you want.

But even the most highly motivated person will have days when things don't flow, old habits surface, motivation wanes. You may find that after some time, you lose some of your momentum. This is very common because a sneaky little thing called resistance may come to call. This can have a big part in your losing your momentum. In this chapter, you will learn the truth about why we lose our motivation, along with some very effective techniques for Maintaining Your Momentum.

Resistance

We would rather be ruined than changed,
We would rather die in our dread

Than climb the cross of the moment
And let our illusions die.
-W. H. Auden

No matter how much you believe that you want to achieve your goal, when the action that you need to take is not within your comfort zone, you will experience resistance. This is the single greatest predictor as to why people give up on their goals.

What is resistance? Put simply, resistance is the reaction we have to any circumstance that is different than what we want it to be. That is, anything that we must do that feels uncomfortable, from having to go to the gym when we would rather be eating a banana split in front of the TV, to having to make a large, risky financial investment to start the business of our dreams, to having to confront an addictive and destructive behaviour we may have been denying, will cause resistance. Understand how to deal with resistance and you have unlocked the most powerful key to goal attainment.

A drastic example of resistance is when we lose a loved one and we feel pain, anger or anguish as part of our grief at the loss. We would give anything to have that person back and we feel tremendous suffering because we so desperately want the situation to be different than it is. We do not want to accept *what is*, and *what is* is that we do not get to have that person in our lives anymore. We do not want to accept that they are gone. We do not want the circumstance to be what it is. We are in resistance.

Of course, this is a very natural and normal reaction to something like death. And as time goes on, and we continue to go through the grieving process, most of us find peace with the loss and accept it. Though we may not like it, we begin to accept it is what is and we do not have the control to make it any different. We are no longer fighting with reality and we accept the circumstance as it is. Peace comes because we are no longer fighting with reality.

In the case of losing a loved one, resistance is easy to understand. But when it comes to taking action toward your goals, you will also find yourself feeling resistance. This seems bizarre because your goal is what you sincerely believe you want. And yet resistance shows up. You don't take the action you said you would. You find an excuse to procrastinate. You tell yourself you don't really have do all these things in order to reach your goal, when deep down, you know that you really do have to take the action you committed to for achieving the goal. Resistance is sneaky and it unquestionably gets in the way of your achieving your goals. Do not underestimate how strong your resistance to achieving your goals can be. But you can overcome resistance.

Why Do We Have Resistance?

Obviously we can understand why we might resist something as painful as the death of someone we care about. But why would we resist achieving the very goals we set for ourselves? The things that we truly believe we want? This seems like some form of insanity. It is not insanity. The truth is that we are hard wired to do so. From an evolutionary point of view, it made sense for us to seek comfort and safety as there were ever-present threats involved with hunting and fighting for survival. We have evolved to avoid pain and discomfort and seek safety and comfort, both physically and emotionally.

This has developed into resistance beyond the things that take us out of our physical or emotional comfort zone. We also have resistance to things that challenge what we believe to be true about ourselves. We do not want things to change. Consistency and predictability are comfortable and safe. And despite what we say we want, we will fight mercilessly to maintain what feels safe and comfortable. This includes what we believe to be true about ourselves. As you read in earlier chapters, the subconscious mind accepts whatever you tell it in a positively or negatively emotionally charged way and, from that, you create a belief that you align your thoughts and actions with. This self-belief (negative or positive) becomes a constantly reinforced neural pathway in your brain that we strongly identify with, even if not in our conscious awareness. This self-belief feels safe and it feels comfortable. What we fail to see now is that being safe and comfortable does not always serve us in our highest good.

Do you want to be in a successful relationship but endlessly seem to attract people who treat you badly? You are in resistance. Despite what you say you want, it is more emotionally comfortable and more in line with your subconscious beliefs about yourself to be in unsuccessful relationships than it is to act out of your comfort zone. Somewhere within your subconscious mind, you do not believe that you can have the relationship you want. Until you work through this resistance, you will continue to create the same situation in slightly different forms, over and over again.

Do you want to make more money but always seem to find yourself in the same mediocre financial situation? You are in resistance. Despite your desire to have more money, it is more emotionally safe and more true to how you subconsciously see yourself to be in the financial situation you are in. Somewhere within your subconscious mind, you don't feel you are capable of making more, or that you are deserving of more, or maybe it is that you believe you are not able to handle more. Until you are able to take action that is uncomfortable because it is not in line with these subconscious beliefs, your financial situation will never grow to what you want it to be.

Do you constantly find yourself losing and gaining the same 10 pounds of weight every time you start to diet? You are in resistance. Despite your dieting, you are more comfortable emotionally being in the cycle of gaining and losing weight. Somewhere within your subconscious mind, you believe that you are not deserving of the body you want or that having that body will mean you no longer have anything to strive for, or perhaps it is that you will attract attention that you cannot handle. Whatever your belief is, until you take action that makes you uncomfortable in order to deal with your resistance, you will continue to struggle with your weight.

Take the endless list of examples of lottery winners who are broke and back to a job at a fast food restaurant within a year or two after winning large sums of money. Why does this happen? It can certainly be argued that they do not have any experience with managing money or they are taken advantage of. But when looking at it from the concept of resistance, people have a subconscious *belief* about what kind of financial status they deserve and they *resist* changing that to the point that they recreate the same financial situation for themselves. This is because it is more comfortable to have the circumstances surrounding them that are in line with their beliefs than it is to change how they see themselves.

This is the same reason that someone like Donald Trump can become virtually bankrupt in the late '80s and early '90s and, within ten years, is worth billions. Donald Trump has a subconscious belief that he is a wildly successful businessman and his beliefs about himself are such that he continually creates circumstances in his life to match them.

Your resistance to change will cause you to create circumstances to line up with your subconscious beliefs about yourself over and over again until you are willing to work through your resistance and change how you see yourself.

Resistance is all about beliefs. Every time you attempt to do something that is not in line with the self-beliefs you have about yourself (positive or negative), you will feel discomfort. As soon as you feel discomfort, you will begin to resist the action you are taking. In order to maintain that hard-wired comfort, you will never step out of the proverbial box.

Let's go back to the example of a goal to make more money. Imagine you have decided your goal is to create an additional $1,500 a month and you have decided your first step in doing so is to ask your boss for a raise. At first you are excited about this idea, and as you begin to think about how much you will ask for, some thoughts creep into your mind:

Am I really worth that much? Maybe my boss will tell me I am pretty nervy asking for a raise when I botched that account last year. I heard Alex asked for a raise last month and he got turned down. I don't want to risk jeopardizing this job in this market by maybe stepping over the line to ask for a raise, especially when my boss may not feel my performance really justifies it. It is too risky. I am doing pretty well at the moment and there are other ways to make extra money. Okay, forget it, there must be another way to bring in some extra income.

Here is an example of how a subconscious belief will keep this person in the same financial situation that he is already in. This is resistance. The subconscious belief is that he doesn't really deserve the raise; he doesn't really deserve more than he has now so he talks himself out of asking. The truth is, he does not know if his boss will say yes or no, but there simply is no way to know until he does something *uncomfortable* that is not already in line with what he believes about himself. He must ask for more money.

What you resist persists.
-Carl Jung

Transforming resistance into action and into success is possible. The trouble is that most people feel resistance and they succumb to the urge to avoid that feeling. Don't. Because what you resist persists. Your resistance is energy and attention directed at the very thing you are resisting, and the more energy you put on something, the bigger you make it. Thus, the more you resist it, the harder is persists. Your resistance causes creative blocks, tension, fighting stress and pain and suffering within you. Resistance is like trying to hold an inflated balloon underwater. It is in opposition to what wants to happen, it is exhausting and it requires your attention. Not only does what you resist persist but it also controls you. It stops you from taking the risks to get out into the world and do the things that make you feel uncomfortable. The thing you are resisting will not go away.

It is time to do something differently than you have done it before. As Einstein said, "insanity: doing the same thing over and over again and expecting a different result." Never underestimate the power of your resistance. But you must also know that once you know how to recognize and deal with your resistance, you control it rather than having it control you.

How to Transform Your Resistance Into Action

Here is how to transform your resistance into action:

1. Honesty

Be truthful with yourself. Are the excuses you are telling yourself for why you are not taking some action step toward your goal really just because it feels uncomfortable? Do you know you can do what it is that you said you were going to do but you really just don't want to feel that discomfort so you are telling yourself stories to justify not doing it? And an even harder question to ask yourself and answer honestly: Do you feel unworthy or undeserving of something? The key to dealing with your resistance in these circumstances is knowing that this is what the excuses are really about. Once you know your excuses and discomfort are just resistance, you can deal with that resistance. As long as you are dishonest with yourself, and you pretend to believe your excuses, you will never work through your resistance and you will hold yourself in the same place that you have always held yourself.

2. Acceptance

Don't fight with your resistance. Accept it is there. It is normal and it probably started as a way to protect you from pain. Everyone, absolutely everyone, has a comfort zone. The second you step out of it, you will feel uncomfortable. This is normal. Accept that you are feeling uncomfortable, that you are experiencing resistance, and notice it. Then simply be ok with resistance showing up.

3. Go Into the Resistance

Once you have accepted that you are feeling resistance, get into how it feels. Do you feel anxious? Where does that sensation show up in your body? Do you feel anger? How does that anger feel physically? Let it wash over you and continue to accept it. Feel it fully and notice that as soon as you do, it dissipates a little. As soon as you feel your resistance, you begin to take its power away.

4. Get Comfortable With Discomfort

As you step out of your comfort zone, resistance rears its ugly head. This is the discomfort that you feel. Simply know that discomfort is just discomfort. It is a requirement of your growth. Get comfortable with having it be there. Feel the resistance and the discomfort and then take the next step anyway.

I remember the first time I was able to use this idea. I noticed, while working on a healthy body goal, my resistance to following my intention to make healthy eating choices when presented with a gooey, sticky, sweet and indulgent-looking cinnamon bun in a café. Rather than find my resistance taking me out of my intended goal, I thought, *I really want to eat that. I really don't want to follow my healthy eating plan. The bad me wants to come out and ruin this better me and I feel this craving and these bad urges and still choose not to eat it anyway.* It was a revelation! I could notice the discomfort and the urges and simply still choose to do something different!

When you begin to get comfortable with your resistance, you can begin to pay attention to the thought processes that go along with it. Once you question those thoughts, resistance becomes much easier to deal with.

5. Forgive Yourself

We can be incredibly hard on ourselves. We will fall into resistance because the patterns in our brain's neural pathways have been strengthened for a very long time through repeated thoughts and behaviours. Doing what we have always done and staying safe is very, very easy and comfortable. You will talk yourself out of taking steps toward your goals. You will find yourself making excuses for choosing actions that do not serve your intended outcome. You will be tempted to fall into the trap of thinking that you have messed up a step and so you may as well just give up.

I call this "potato chip thinking." I love potato chips. I love the crispy, crunchy, salty sensation of them. I love the smell of the oil they are fried in. Potato chips have been one of my naughty foods of choice ever since I can remember. Road trips, DVD nights, camping and parties have always been excuses for me to buy family-sized bags of potato chips, having convinced myself that I will share and then essentially eating the entire bag on my own.

But I know that I have long since left behind the days of being a skinny teenager that could pack away endless bags of potato chips and not gain an ounce of fat. Not to mention the fact that they are a very unhealthy choice of snack. My general policy is to stay away from potato chips. If I refrain, I refrain fully. I feel pretty good about my self-discipline. But if I have just one, I seem to feel that I must then eat the entire bag full.

The thinking is, *well, I screwed this one up, I may as well screw it up as royally as I can.* For me this translates into no potato chips, or the whole bag. When it is a "whole bag" day, I get pretty tempted to beat myself up for it. Self-forgiveness is much more effective of a way to deal with greasy hands and an empty potato chip bag. When I beat myself up, I take a lot longer to get back on track. I feel down on myself. I feel ineffective. This is not a very motivating state from which to reset and get back on course.

When I forgive myself, I am able to wash the grease off my hands, crinkle up the bag, throw it away (along with my guilt and remorse) and recommit to my goal of refraining from potato chips.

One way or another, on the path to achieving your goal, you will have a fabulous screwup. Know that you will eat a potato chip. Know that you may even eat the whole bag. Be gentle with yourself. You are changing long-standing patterns that you may have been practicing since you were five years old. It is ok if you screw up. Forgive yourself, let it go and know that it does not mean you have to give up on the goal. Forgive yourself, reset and get back on course.

What Are You Willing to Give Up?

The self-help industry takes in upwards of ten billion dollars annually in the United States alone. Why are people so willing to spend money on self-help?

Many of you already have a dozen or more self-help books on your shelves. If you have read them, they likely had important or valuable content in them, but have you applied it?

The fact of the matter is that we are inclined to search for a "magic bullet." We buy programs and books and seminars because we want to find the way to get the outcome without doing the work. I am as guilty of this as many of you are. I have been watching TV late at night and been convinced that I would finally have the toned, flat stomach that I had dreamed of for so long once I got that great special offer on one of those exercise devices that vaguely resemble torture devices from Medieval Europe. Out comes the credit card, and lo and behold, a year later it is an awkward-to-store frame in the corner. And instead of having washboard abs, the special offer exercise contraption is covered in my drying laundry.

The truth is that there are many great programs out there and the DREAM Power Goal System is one of them. It works, every time, guaranteed, *if you do the work.*

Now, you have likely figured this out by now. You may be feeling very inspired and excited about the goals you plan to accomplish with the powerful tools that have been presented to you here. You have read all about how sneaky and powerful resistance is and how to handle your resistance. You may even be jumping up and down because you have begun to take action and you have seen some results already (which I truly hope you have!). Here is the catch: the reality of it is that *in order to do the work* and create the results that you want, you have to be willing to give some things up.

1. Giving Up Negative Self-Beliefs

The first things that you need to be willing to give up are your negative self-beliefs. Easy! Great! Who would not want to give up negative self-beliefs? But we are more attached to these than you might like to think! Our negative self-beliefs would not be in place in our subconscious if they did not have a payoff. There is a reward for constantly creating situations to prove our negative self-beliefs true. Most negative self-talk that we do comes down to a root of one of the following three negative self-beliefs: I am not capable, I am not lovable and I am not deserving. Let's have a look at the payoffs for believing these.

I am not capable/ lovable /deserving

Payoff: You get to **blame** your lack of capability, lovability or worthiness on the people you believe caused you to feel incapable, unlovable or unworthy for your life situation.

Payoff: You get to **blame** your lack of capability, lovability or worthiness on the fact that you do not have the goals you want in life.

Payoff: You don't have to step out of your comfort zone.

Payoff: You get to feel **comfortable**.

Payoff: You get to **stay safe**.

Payoff: You get **excuses** for why you are where you are.

Payoff: You get **sympathy and attention** from others for your failings and circumstances.

You must be willing to give up these payoffs so that you can get out of your own way and use the DREAM Power Goal System!

So, what does giving up these payoffs look like? What would your life be like if you did not live this way?

Blame

When you give up blame, blaming becomes knowing you are responsible for what you have created because you have been the only one to choose the actions you have taken and the beliefs that you have chosen to believe. Blame becomes personal responsibility. Personal responsibility is empowerment. If someone else is responsible, you do not have control. If you are responsible, you have control. Only with a sense of personal responsibility can we take ownership of our goals and know that we are in control of what kind of outcomes we create.

Comfort and Safety

When you give up comfort and safety, they become willingness to take risks. Comfort and safety allow us to avoid feeling afraid, awkward, rejected or hurt. They help us to avoid losing what we already have. Without the willingness to take the risk of feeling afraid, awkward, rejected or hurt, or without being willing to lose what we already have, we do not give ourselves the opportunity to feel deep love, experience powerful connections, achieve big dreams, make lots of money, develop our self-understanding and grow. Only with big risks can we potentially create big rewards.

Excuses

When you give up excuses, you stop spending time justifying the position you are in and you begin to keep your word to yourself and others. Excuses are another way to avoid personal responsibility for your choices and to let yourself out of the commitments that you make to yourself and others. When you stop making excuses, you begin to accept responsibility and to keep your word. This creates a sense of personal integrity. Only with this strong personal integrity can we begin to change our sense of self worth and self-esteem. When that happens, we believe that we are worthy and deserving of the goals we want to create.

Sympathy and Attention

When you give up seeking out sympathy and attention for your negative choices and behaviour, you free up a lot of space and energy for other things. You begin to see that the bottomless pit of neediness will never be filled by the sympathy and attention of others. In fact, the very act of seeking this holds you in the pattern of your life that you are in. It is only when you give up the need for sympathy and attention from others, and take action toward what you know you want in your life, that you will attract empowering support in your life and people will want to help you move forward instead of feeling sorry for you.

2. Giving Up Approval From Others

If you really want to go for your goals, you will find people who will disapprove. This may come in an outright statement of disapproval from someone in your life for your choice of goal because it stands in contrast to the values of your family, religion, culture or community. Set yourself up with the awareness of the fact that people you care about may disapprove of your choice. If you are expecting the possibility of disapproval, it is much easier to deal with than if you are not.

Disapproval may come in much sneakier forms too. When you begin to take action in your life, others may feel threatened that your relationship with them will change. Some people may also be reacting to their own knowledge inside that they too want to achieve their goals but they do not want to have to take action. Your choice to change your own life frightens them. So instead, they naysay your ideas, highlight what you might lose by taking the risks you need to take to achieve your goals, focus on your obstacles or provide some other unsupportive reaction. They are disapproving not because they do not believe in you, but because of what it means for them.

Know that you might well upset people when you reach for what you truly want in your life. This can be brutally difficult to do, especially if you have been a people-pleaser for most of your life, as I have. If you need the approval of others, you will find yourself in conflict with your choices and what those other people want for you. Your need for approval will hold you back from taking steps in the direction that you really want to go. When you get clear within yourself that your goals are more important than the approval of others, you can really begin to move forward. You will find, more often than not, that you will eventually gain their respect. You will also be amazed at the fact that when you align your behaviours with what you truly want and not what others want for you, your sense of self will shift. You will feel great about yourself! And that, in turn, will motivate you to continue to take steps in the direction of your goals.

3. Giving Up Laziness

Laziness plagues me. I can have the best intention to sit right down and do some work toward my goals for my entire journey home from work and, as soon as I get home, I look over at my cozy couch, my blanket and the TV remote and feel called to them. I justify going over to that couch with a glass of wine in hand, "I worked hard today. I *deserve* this. I'll just have one glass of wine and watch one TV show and then I will get to work."

But I know now, that once I am down on that couch, I am down. It is my laziness place; it is a black hole where time disappears and warm fuzzies engulf me. I absolutely know that I have to give up the lazy couch lolling if I want to achieve my goals.

You must be willing to give up laziness if you suffer from it (or enjoy it) like I do. It is not my intention to imply that laziness is inherently wrong. I really do enjoy a lazy afternoon reading a book with a cup of tea on the couch, avoiding the responsibilities of life. But what you must become clear on is that you are giving up one, albeit possibly enjoyable, period of time in order to do something that gives a higher reward in the long run.

4. Giving Up the Way It Is Supposed to Look

You must be willing to give up having it look the way you think it is supposed to look. What does this mean? It means that you have your goal in mind. You have what you think you need to do, the support you think you need to get and the action that you believe you need to take mentally scripted for yourself. This is great. You are clear and on the road to achieving your goals! But you may find that you have become attached to doing it, whatever it is that you are doing, the way you *think* it needs to be done.

One of the most common ways this shows up is when people have a goal to create a certain amount of money in a given time period. When I began looking for ways to create the down payment for my first home, I had this idea that I was going to earn it by running a small tutoring business on the side and spending less of my regular income. I had played with the numbers and I could bring in quite a bit of extra cash if I were to tutor groups rather than individuals. I spent quite a bit of time planning and figuring out how to attract the students, how I would set up the program, what I needed to do to start a small side business and so on. I even bought a domain name and researched how to create my own website. My efforts were almost fruitless. Although I did attract a few more one-on-one clients, no one signed up for my program. I was deflated and frustrated because the money was not coming to me and I was so sure that this was going to be my big money maker.

While I was spending all the time and energy on this project, I had been offered the opportunity to help out a friend to sell some things that he had acquired at cost and did not really have the time to deal with. He really wanted them off his hands and said that I could keep 50 percent of any profit I made on them. But I had been saying *no* to his offer because I did not think I was any good at sales. It was not until I was in a Mastermind group where someone pointed out that perhaps I was expecting the money to come the way *I* thought it was supposed to that it dawned on me that I had *nothing to lose* by taking my friend up on his offer. My time investment would be as much as taking ads out on <u>craigslist.org</u> and being home when people wanted to come by and check out the items. Why was I saying no to the opportunity that was right in front of my eyes?

I took my friend up on the offer and made a few thousand dollars in a month on the sale of his items! I had been resisting this and it had been easy! I completely let go of my attachment to money needing to show up the way I thought it had to and, after that, I suddenly began to see possibilities to make extra cash everywhere. Once I did that, I was able to create the money I needed for my down payment within a matter of about five weeks.

Another area that people have ideas about the way it is supposed to look is the support that they have around them. For example, many people expect that their significant other should be their main support. They feel frustrated and angry when their husband or wife is not being supportive of their goal. The truth is that their partner either will or won't support them the way they want. If their partner will not, they may get so caught up in their frustration about this that they neglect to see a good friend who is calling to check in on how their goal is going. Rather than see the support they are being offered, they will use the phone call to complain about their partner who is not living up to their expectations.

We must be willing to give up the way we think it is supposed to look. This means ... are you ready for it? Letting go of the notion that you will control it all. When you can let go of your desire to control how it will look, you can let go of your expectations. When you let go of your expectations, you can begin to see other possibilities exist that may be much better than the ones you thought you were going to see. When you give up controlling how it is supposed to look, you open up to infinite possibilities for how it can look.

Let me be clear. I do not think that you can literally just give up all your negative self-beliefs, need for approval, laziness and expectations for how things should look after reading the last few pages. It is a process. But the key here is that you now have these in your conscious awareness. So now you can begin to give up these hindrances from taking action. You can be prepared for when you find them coming up and simply acknowledge to yourself that they are there, that they do not serve you and that it is going to be a push. Perhaps it will be rather uncomfortable at first, but you can simply choose to do something differently and continue to take more and more effective action toward your goals!

Commitment

Commitment is the enemy of resistance, for it is the serious promise to press on, to get up, no matter how many times you are knocked down.
-David McNally

Get committed. Of the 10 percent or so of people who actually do write down their goals, an even smaller percentage go on to actually achieve them. You have written down your goals. You are already ahead of 90 percent of the population. This is a huge step! Focus on this as a success! What stops the entire 10 percent of people who write down their goals from actually going on to achieve them is resistance. We have looked at resistance at length and you can see that resistance, in all its sneaky ways, can be overcome. But what that requires is commitment.

You must be absolutely committed to your goals. You must be willing to do what it takes to get to your desired outcome. This is your work. Know that your resistance is really just a series of illusions and negative thoughts. When you know that although it may be uncomfortable, you absolutely can get through the resistance, you truly become unstoppable! With a clear vision of what you want, the intention to get it and commitment, supported by the tools in this book, there is nothing that you cannot achieve.

It is very easy to say that you are committed to your goals when you are not feeling resistance. And you may take big, powerful steps toward the life of your dreams when you are energized, full of excitement and feeling great. You must be grateful for these times and ride this wave for as long as you can by using these tools. But when the resistance comes and you want to give up, your commitment is your word to yourself that you will follow through.

Take a moment to consider that. Your commitment is your word to yourself that you will follow through and do what you say. Think about people you know that do not do what they say; people who do not walk their talk. These are the people who say they will come to an event and cancel at the last minute or do not show up. These are the people who claim that honesty is to be valued but whom you catch in a little white lie. How do you feel about them? What is the subtle sense you have about whether or not you can really trust them? Are they the people whom you would turn to when you needed to count on someone? You know how you feel about these people, but yet you may not be keeping your word to yourself. What does this reflect to you about how you value yourself?

When you give your word to someone else, what does your word mean to you? This is a representation of your integrity. Most people, when they give their word to someone else, will move mountains to keep it, but they are much more likely to break their word to themselves. Making a commitment to your goals is your opportunity to keep your word to yourself. This is a gift to yourself. Hold yourself to the standard of integrity that you would hold yourself to as if the commitment was to another. Who can be more valuable to yourself than you? Give yourself the same worth that you hold for others. Keep your commitment to yourself and watch how your view of yourself changes.

Take the time now to write down your commitment to your goals. Again, this might feel a bit frightening because it means that you have to do it, but if you really want it, what would stop you? Your resistance is only a reflection of habitual thoughts that do not serve you. This is your opportunity to do something different that will shift your consciousness about yourself and propel you to the next level of your life! Go for it. Do it now. Get seriously committed!

Perseverance

In the confrontation between the stream and the rock, the stream always wins – not through strength but through perseverance.
-H. Jackson Brown

Obviously, perseverance is required in order to maintain your commitment. Again, it is easy to say that you will persevere and persist when things are going well. And again, be grateful and love those times when you have them. There is nothing like the bliss of moving forward with momentum into a world of success. Revel in it!

The challenge, of course, comes when you are faced with a rejection, failure or course interruption. This is difficult in the best of times, but when you have taken a step out of your "box" and into a space that feels out of control and overwhelming and you have a setback like rejection, you better believe you are going to want to crawl back into that box, pull the lid down tight, turn off the lights and hide from that nasty out-of-the-box world where you felt spurned.

When this happens, and it will if you are truly taking risks, take some time and lick your wounds if you need to. But then check back in with your commitment to yourself. Know that you now have one very effective method for not getting what you want. That is really all it is. Your bruised ego will want to make up all kinds of stories about your worthiness, your ineffectiveness, the big bad world being out to get you and how safe and comfortable you are inside rather than outside of your box. But, again, these are just habitual thoughts that do not serve you. When you check back in with your commitment to yourself and know that there is a way to get what you are trying to get (you just haven't found it yet), go back to perseverance. Try something different. Yes, you have to open the lid of the box and step out again. Yes, it could go wrong again, but perseverance is about the faith that you will get there if you keep trying. As Dale Carnegie, the author of the massive best seller *How to Win Friends and Influence People* (which was published in 1936 and still remains popular today for its practical and effective messages), said, "Most of the important things in the world have been accomplished by people who have kept on trying when there seemed to be no hope at all."

You will face obstacles that seem practically, physically or emotionally insurmountable. If there were no obstacles, you would have what you wanted already! The bigger your goal, the bigger the obstacles will be. Hold the vision of your goal achieved in your mind. Use the tools in previous chapters to take action and then connect with your commitment and your integrity and persevere. You will achieve anything that you want to.

Trust the Process

When things are going as we want or expect them to, it is easy to trust that what is happening is the right thing. This propels your momentum. When they are not, when those obstacles come up or the results do not come as we expect them to, we may begin to question the process. This can be a momentum killer.

The DREAM Power Goal System works. But you must be willing to trust the process. Consider the metaphor of the seed again. Let's have the seed represent the visualized completed goal being planted in your subconscious mind. Every action you take, from any step in the DREAM Power Goal System, is water or fertilizer for that seed. The seed needs some germination time. But if you continue to persist with your commitment to your goal when nothing seems to be happening, and the obstacles keep presenting themselves to you, your persistence will pay off. This is because even though you do not see the sprout breaking through the soil, there are biochemical reactions happening below the visible surface that mean that seed is about to burst through the ground. But if you give up because you have not seen your results yet and stop watering and feeding your seed it will never grow. Water and feed your seed with the tools presented here and trust that under the visible surface growth is occurring. Before you know it, a bud will emerge.

This is what it means to trust the process. Even though you cannot see the results initially, if you trust that what you are doing is working, you are metaphorically stimulating the metabolism of your seed so that it can germinate and you will get results. Your plant will grow. Your goal will be achieved.

Wayne Dyer, an author who has a tremendous impact in my life, put it this way: "You will see it when you believe it." In fact, this was the title of one of his first best sellers.

I remember the first time I heard this, because it literally turns the old notion of "I will believe it when I see it" on its head and to me. It was completely empowering. I could take action before my circumstances changed just by changing my thoughts. Learning from Wayne Dyer that I had to believe it *before* I would see it affected my thinking profoundly and allowed me to take some of the steps I did when I was looking for my dream job referred to in the Introduction. If I had not had faith that my new thoughts, visualizations and actions would work during those tough times being unemployed, lonely and broke, I simply would have given up on doing them. I may have given up on getting a teaching job altogether. I would have used the lack of results as evidence that my thoughts, visualizations and actions were *not* working!

But instead, I had absolute faith that I would achieve that dream job and it took many months of watering the seed, but I never gave up. I trusted the process and I got everything I wanted, and more!

Most of us have this wrong. We think that the results must come before the belief. This will *not* get you results, or at least it will not get you the results that you want, and it will be a way for you to provide evidence for yourself that following the steps in this book do not work. Your faith *must* come first. Trust that the processes work. Believe that you will find the way to create what you want and you will. Know that every time you visualize, every time you state your gratitude for achieving your goal (even though you don't have it yet), every time you jump up and down and energize yourself, every positive action you take toward achieving your goal, big or small, you are watering the seed that you have planted.

Get Support

Mastermind

We have all heard the expression that two minds are better than one. It is absolutely true. This is because your habitual ways of thinking are so engrained that you simply do not even realize that you may be subconsciously judging and editing out creative ideas that could be the solutions to your obstacles. You are blinded from seeing them as possibilities. Discussing your obstacles with other people and then being open to hearing their ideas is a very powerful process to keep you moving toward your goals when you are feeling stuck.

The Mastermind group is a way of working with others to support your movement through resistance and toward your goals. A Mastermind group is a group of people who are like-minded and actively pursuing their goals. This group meets regularly and offers support to each other. Mastermind groups work through the concept of synergy.

Take this example: When I was working on my goal of purchasing my first home, I did not have enough money for a down payment. I was also in debt, so borrowing it was not an option. I had to come up with a solution for creating several thousand dollars in cash. This seemed totally impossible to me. My salary was not going to change, my savings account was miserably non-existent and no one I knew was likely to hand me several thousand in cash! Where was I going to get this money from?

I did belong to a Mastermind group at the time and so I asked for support with this. We set our Mastermind group up in such a way that when someone had an obstacle they were stuck on, they would present the problem until everyone was clear on it and then the person with the problem had to shut up. Literally. They could not say a single word while everyone else threw out ideas. At the same time, someone would scribe all the ideas that came up.

Why was the person with the problem not allowed to speak? So that they could not vocalize all the spontaneous responses based in resistance that would likely come up. They could not explain why there was no possibility of it. It allowed them to stay open to possibilities that they had not previously considered.

My experience with this process was very powerful. The list of things that people came up with had many things on it that I considered ridiculous. As a generally verbose person, staying quiet was difficult at the best of times, but when people were suggesting money-generating ideas that were way out of my box, the urge to explain why they would never work was very strong! But because I had to sit there silently, not dismissing the ideas, I slowly began to "hear" them and, additionally, to consider them. Some of the things that were suggested to me, that I would never have come up with on my own, I ended up using very effectively to help me generate the cash that I needed. I am incredibly grateful for my Mastermind group.

Anyone can start a Mastermind group. Connect with people who are like-minded and set up some expectations for the group and then meet weekly.

Support Buddies

A support buddy (or goal buddy) is anyone who will support you in achieving your goals. Ideally, a goal buddy is not someone who may feel threatened by the changes that you will make. If they have been an accomplice in your ineffective behaviours in the past, have been someone who has not held you to your word or who is not particularly motivated themselves, they are probably not a good choice as a support buddy.

A true support buddy will push you and hold you accountable when you are in resistance, up against big obstacles or losing your motivation. Support buddies can be friends, coworkers or family members. Support buddies can also be found through *Meetup* groups. *Meetup* (www.meetup.com) is an online social networking portal that facilitates offline group meetings in various localities around the world. If you don't know about *Meetup*, it is a great tool for finding people who are interested in the same things you are.

However you find your buddy, you will need to be very honest and clear about what kind of support you are looking for. Tell your buddy that you want to be held accountable to your goal. Ask them if they think that they will know how to challenge you when they think you might be feeding them stories and excuses about why you are not taking action. Support is an undeniably important part of maintaining your momentum.

Coaches and Experts

Another powerful way to create support in your life is to hire someone to work with you. Hiring someone to work with you in achieving your goals adds a new layer of commitment to your desired outcome. We place a very high value on money. When you invest in yourself, you are sending a message to yourself that you are very serious about what you intend to create. You expect a return on your investment and, in this case, that return is a better you. Investing money in your growth will drive you to really step up to the plate. Not only are you creating a support person in your life who is solely dedicated to your success, and has no hidden agenda in his or her support of you, but if you spent money on it, you will be far more likely to show up for your support meetings. You will be far more likely to take those action steps that you set out for yourself because you know you are not just accountable to yourself, but you are also accountable to someone else. On top of all that, you receive the benefit of working with someone who has expertise in supporting people in achieving their goals. There are no shortage of people offering support services out there. Do some research, find someone who is a good match for you and create support to keep Maintain Your Momentum.

Re-Energize!

When all else fails, and momentum is slipping, shift your energy from pain to power. The following techniques could have been included in the Energize chapter but I have saved them for Maintaining your Momentum because they are wonderful ways to propel yourself out of a motivation slump.

Get Out of Your Comfort Zone

One of the quickest ways to shift your energy and get your momentum going again is to step out of your comfort zone and take a risk. If this is something that can be tied to your goals, even better. But it does not need to be. Here are some ideas that successful goal getters I know have used in order to boost their energy and excitement about life to jump start themselves when they have become stuck.

Physical Energizers

These will make you feel alive again! Go out and try one of these or take a lesson. Your heart will be racing and you will be ready to take on the world!

* Go-cart Racing
* Paintballing
* Bungee Jumping
* Skydiving
* Rock Climbing
* Kite Boarding

Social and Emotional Energizers

Feel the thrill of connecting with others by taking some social and emotional risks. These will make the people you involve feel wonderful and the effect it has on you will get you revved up and invigorated. You will wonder why you don't do these things all the time!

* Ask a stranger out on a date
* Stand on a street corner and see how many free hugs you can give away
* Leave a ridiculously large tip for a server in a restaurant
* Buy the person behind you in line a coffee at your local café
* Anonymously leave your neighbours boxes of chocolates outside their doors
* Buy a dozen long-stemmed roses and give them away to people on a busy street who look like they need to be cheered up

* Drop by a local retirement community and visit with elderly people and just listen to their stories
* Write a heartfelt letter of forgiveness, love or gratitude to someone you know you really owe it to

Once you engage in a few triggers to get your momentum going again, you will feel alive and ready to tackle your goals with gusto!

Summary

M is for Maintain Your Momentum in The DREAM Power Goal System

Maintaining Your Momentum is the last step in manifesting your goals into reality. You will find slumps in your momentum, but use the understandings you gain here about why most people give up and apply the tools and techniques for dealing with them. This will help you empower yourself to see your goals through to fruition.

Resistance

When you feel the momentum for your goals dipping, this is coming from your resistance. Your resistance is a force to be reckoned with but it is not unsurpassable. Your resistance comes from the fact that you have subconscious negative self-beliefs about your worthiness, capability and/or lovability. You can push through your resistance by confronting it with honesty, acceptance, allowance, willingness to get uncomfortable and forgiveness. When you acknowledge and accept the resistance, you can choose to do what it is that you need to take action on despite it.

What Are You Willing to Give Up?

To create results with the DREAM Power Goal System, you have to work the work. In order to do so, you need to become willing to give up your negative self-beliefs and all of their hidden payoffs. You need to become willing to give up approval from others, laziness and your attachment to the way it is supposed to look. When you become willing to give these up, you get out of your own way. When you get out of your own way, your momentum is unstoppable.

Commitment and Perseverance

Commitment and perseverance go without saying when it comes to Maintaining Your Momentum. Commitment is easy when things are flowing in the direction of your goals and you are not feeling resistance. As soon as resistance comes, however, you may find that your commitment is waning. Consider what committing to yourself means. Get committed to keeping your word to yourself with the same integrity as if you gave your word to another. Simply keeping your word to yourself when you commit to your goals will have a profound effect on your self-esteem and thrust you even faster in the direction of your dreams. When you are categorically committed to your goal, perseverance comes naturally. The more risks you take, the more likely you will get knocked off the proverbial horse. Persevere! Check in with your commitment and get back on the horse!

Trust the Process

Do not despair when you do not see results right away, even though you are doing the work. You could be around the corner from a huge shift forward but if you give up, it will not have the chance to appear! The DREAM Power Goal System works, every time, guaranteed. Trust the process and persevere and you will create the results you want.

Get Support

A wonderful way to **Maintain Your Momentum** is to create support in your life. Surround yourself with people who are moving in a similar direction and are willing to support you. Create a Mastermind group, where like-minded people problem solve synergistically to **Maintain** the **Momentum** of the goal seekers in the group. Find a support buddy–someone who will hold you accountable to what you say you will do and who will not buy your excuses. Hire an expert or coach. Investing in your own success financially is a powerful way to boost your belief in your own worth and to create very motivating support.

Get Out of Your Comfort Zone

When momentum is lagging and you need to kick it up a notch or two, do something that is fun and exciting outside of your comfort zone. Take a physical or social risk that will energize you. This may or may not be something that moves you closer to your goal but it doesn't matter. The shift that will occur in you physically will restart your engines and get you racing again toward your goals!

You are there. In the DREAM Power Goal System, you have all the tools and techniques required to get any goal! Apply them religiously and watch yourself create anything that you want!

A Final Word
Your Greater Vision

Cherish your visions and your dreams as they are the children of your soul; the blueprint of your ultimate achievements.
–Napolean Hill

Everyone has big and small goals that they would like to achieve. These will evolve and change as your life does so. Now that you have successfully taken the DREAM Power concepts from this book, applied them to some goals and used them to achieve any goal, you now know that you have an incredibly powerful system that you can use to create absolutely anything that you dream of!

You may have already begun your next set of goals to work on. Fantastic! Go for it! Achieve everything that you want in your life. This system will support you if you stick to it and use the strategies of the DREAM Power Goal System.

Your Vision

Now I want to challenge you to go beyond your goals. And let me reinforce the fact that I absolutely support you to continue to achieve any goal you desire. But aren't our goals really just stepping-stones to our greater vision?

Your greater vision is related to your sense of purpose in life. Consistently happy people are very often connected to their purpose and, thus, they have a vision about how they want their life to be that is then broken into goals that they work to achieve. If you are already connected to your purpose, you are very lucky. Many people do not really know how to find their purpose and, therefore, float along, working at a job that is ok (or that they hate), achieving individual goals (or not even getting as far as setting goals) and feeling an overall mild (or worse) sense of dissatisfaction with their life.

People who are connected to purpose have a vision for how that purpose will play out in their lives. They hold that vision clearly in their minds. Then they can see the direction they're headed in and what goals they need to achieve to get there. Goal setting becomes much easier and the motivation, with the driving vision behind it, increases!

Recently, I was working with a volunteer group and, as a perk to the volunteers, the coordinator wanted to coach us on our purpose, vision and goals. We started with stating our goals. Mine was that toned, flat belly that I have mentioned once or twice before in this book as something I desire. Then the coordinator asked us what we would do if we had the perfect body, all the money we wanted already in the bank and great relationships with the ones we loved. Everyone started to think. What really mattered to us beyond those material and immediate gratification goals? When it was my turn to speak, I found myself quite choked up. I said that I wanted to make a difference in people's lives by inspiring them to get in touch with what they don't believe that they can achieve for themselves.

The coordinator told me that my tears meant that I had hit something deep for me. That when tears come, we are tapping into our real purpose. He wanted to know how I was going to do it, what my exact vision was. The words came out before I knew what I was going to say. "I'm going to publish a book that will change people's lives."

And just like that, I knew that my flat, toned belly was not really all that important to me right then. My purpose was to help people change their lives. My vision was to do so through a book and my goals were going to be around getting the book researched, written and published.

How do you connect with your greater vision and purpose? Get out a piece of paper and a pen or open your laptop. Answer the question below with as many answers as come up. Write a hundred if that is how many ideas come up for you. Note how you feel as you write each one. Don't edit yourself, even if you think your answer is not what you should write. It does not have to be something dramatic or noble. Oprah Winfrey, in her final episode of her show, made reference to the best facial she ever had and the clinician told her that it was the best facial that Oprah had ever had because the clinician was passionate about popping zits! She knew her purpose—beautiful skin.

Here is the question:

What would you do if you did not have to work for money?

Once you have written your answers, go back and circle the ones that made you feel emotional. If they made you cry, you are really onto something.

If you did not find yourself really connecting to any of the things that you wrote, don't worry. You do have a purpose. Everyone does. Just start to notice what you are attracted to. What charities do you, or would you like to, support? What type of books do you enjoy most? What type of activities get you excited? What type of people do you prefer to spend your time around? If you had a chance to go back to university and study anything you wanted, what would it be? If you want to find your purpose, you will find it.

Once you have a sense of your purpose, you can begin to envision your ideal world based on that purpose. Oprah's clinician might have had a vision of owning her own chain of spas where people could get the best-quality treatments available. Someone whose purpose is to help women living on the street may have a vision of starting a shelter where women can learn skills for employment and where they feel safe and supported. Someone whose purpose is to dance may have a vision of dancing for the Royal Ballet in Britain. Someone whose purpose is to heal the sick may have a vision of becoming a director for Doctors Without Borders.

Create this greater vision in your life as your ideal situation—what your dream world would be if you had the power to create it. Just like with your goal setting at the beginning of the book, you do not need to know how you are going to do this, you just need to know that you feel passionate about it.

When you have created your vision, based around your purpose, goals that are stepping-stones toward your vision become much easier to define.

I want to leave you with a call to find that deeper passion that lies within you. I will always support people in setting and achieving any goal because I believe we can create whatever we choose for ourselves. But I also know that beyond those goals, we have a calling, something within us that is our gift to the world. That ultimate purpose wants to come forward but we often hide from it because of the risks involved in really taking this purpose on.

Our deepest fear is not that we are inadequate. Our deepest fear is that we are powerful beyond measure. It is our light, not our darkness that most frightens us. We ask ourselves, Who am I to be brilliant, gorgeous, talented, fabulous? Actually, who are you not to be? You are a child of God. Your playing small does not serve the world.
-Marianne Williamson

Go within and find out what blessing you really know exists inside you, and connect to that greater vision. Your soul will thank you as it is beckoning to be allowed to express itself through you. Give yourself and the world that gift.

Want More?

Take advantage of a **special offer** from Monica.

Sign up for a **complimentary strategy session** on putting the *DREAM Power Goal System* to use in your life today!

Simply go to:
dreampowergoal.com

This complimentary 30 minute strategy session could change your life!

Also available on the DREAM Power Goal System website:

» **Find Action Plan Templates** for putting the DREAM Power Goal System into practice.

» **Read articles and check out resources** to support you on your journey to your goal.

» **Download your FREE MP3 Audio** that reveals the secret to why you have struggled to successfully achieve your goals and what you can do to start overcoming your struggle today! — *Value $59.00*

» **Receive a complimentary subscription to the "DREAM Power – Inspiration Newsletter."**

And much more!

CPSIA information can be obtained at www.ICGtesting.com
Printed in the USA
LVOW010355200911

246961LV00004B/3/P